SOME PERFECT
TOMORROW

SOME PERFECT TOMORROW

TRUE STORIES OF HOPE IN LOSS, LOVE IN GRIEF, AND LIFE IN DEATH

CRAIG R. SEATON

YELLORONDACK PUBLISHING

PUBLISHED BY YELLORONDACK PUBLISHING

PAPERBACK ISBN · 9781736039205
Front Cover Image and Photo by Chloé Austin
Cover and Interior Designed by Leslie M. Browning
Edited by R. Alan Clanton and S.D. Michael,
with special thanks to Lynn Skapyak Harlin.

Printed in the United States of America
10 9 8 7 6 5 4 3 2 1

Acknowledgements

Thank you.
To the One who holds my molecules together;
the Family who holds me together;
Tami, Tylor, Tara, Dennis, Frances,
David, Shawn, Matt, and Tonya;
the Thousands whose paths hold mine together;
and to the few who held my words together:
T. Deering Manning, Mark Malatesta, Alan Clanton,
S.D. Michael, and finally, Lynn Skapyak Harlin,
who taught me which of those words belong on a page.

Contents

For Tami.
The wife of my youth.

Foreword
by R. Alan Clanton

For all human history death has been the great mystery. We must all face our mortality, and the mortality of others at some stage in our lives.

One day we will likely lose friends, family, and loved ones. As survivors, we will experience a variety of emotions, challenges, and new realities brought about by these deaths.

No matter what anyone tells you—pastor, priest, imam, rabbi, counselor, author, talk-show expert, friend or family member—there is no playbook. No template. No rulebook. No user-friendly digital app for how we cope with such profound loss.

Death affects us in ways we cannot predict or foresee. Though it often helps to visualize the healing process as linear, as if the straight highway of time alone will heal. The complexity of what we feel is more akin to a tapestry.

Emotions and uncertainty mixing with blame. Feelings of emptiness, regret, relief, and grief. Grief is the tough part. Unlike mourning, which should not go on forever. Grief can last a lifetime.

Craig Seaton has drawn on his decades of experience as a professional dealing with death and grief. *Some Perfect*

Tomorrow is a compelling and joyfully diverse look at how we can learn to adjust to the changed realities brought about by the death of a loved one. As these richly varied and often strikingly different examples show, there are no set rules for the pain. No deadlines for the heart.

Each relationship we have in this world is unlike the next. Our experience comes by way of different circumstances. Our reactions and adjustments, too, must vary.

The wisdom in this book will help even before you experience a loss. Change the way you look at others. The immense personal value of empathy. The mysterious driving force of hope. Both can greatly improve our lives. Today and tomorrow.

Craig approaches each of his real-world stories with respect and dignity. Each short chapter ends with Sparks of Life—points to think about as you let the story sink in. These will help you navigate your own grief. The author caringly weaves each intimate account using his well-tuned sense of timing, his remarkable observational skills, and yes, even his whimsical, charming sense of humor.

Perhaps this is Craig's point. Death is a certainty in this life, and the complexities of the pain and grief are powerful. Yet we can navigate the choppy survivor's sea with a touch of joy in our hearts and maybe even a smile on our faces.

—R. Alan Clanton
Editor, *Thursday Review*
Author, *Conversations Overheard in a Restaurant*

Introduction

I F I TOLD YOU, "I KNOW HOW YOU FEEL," I'D BE LYING.
If I let you know, "I understand," you'd be doubtful.
If I said, "I've been there," we'd both just smile.

In the truest sense, I don't know how you feel; I don't understand, and I've not been exactly where you are. But I'm compelled to share with you how I've felt, what I've understood, and where I've been—in the hope somehow you can make sense of an impossible task like losing someone close to you. Why?

Because you matter. You make a difference in the world. You're important. The Merriam-Webster dictionary defines important as, "being marked by or indicative of significant worth; valuable in content or relationship."

Merriam-Webster just described you. You're important because you were important to them, to the someone you lost—and that still matters. It will always matter.

Just because you've experienced loss doesn't mean the relationship with the person ends. When someone close to us dies, it drives us into something deeper than simply realizing we no longer have them with us in the flesh. Losing someone we love permeates every fiber of our being—mentally, emotionally, spiritually, even physically. Their absence creates a dark insatiable abyss, and it hurts like crazy.

Memories can be healing one moment and shattering the next. I'm convinced these same memories can be your redemption—mine have been for me.

When my dad died in 1998, I never knew just how much losing someone could hurt. I loved my dad with all my heart and his death rocked me deep inside. But losing my mother twelve years later left me crippled.

We grieve to the extent we love someone. I guess I love my parents a lot. I'll limp a little for the rest of my life. This doesn't mean I can no longer walk. It's just my gait is slightly different than before I lost them. If you've lost someone you love, you know what I'm talking about.

Yes, we must get back up and begin to live again, and this book will help you. But to think life will ever look the same again is to fool ourselves. It will never look the same and that's okay. You can still live and love, give and take, breathe in, and breathe out, and learn to walk again.

Grief is a strange houseguest. It doesn't seem to care when it comes to visit, how long it stays, or even if it sits in your favorite chair. Unwelcomed or not, grief is going to drop by your house sooner or later. When it does, it helps to know you're not the only one on its agenda. Others are grieving too. Just knowing this one truth may be salvation enough.

There's something beautifully and innately human about our need to share thoughts and experiences with other humans. It's helpful in a self-therapeutic way—for both the teller and the hearer—letting us know we're not losing our minds with all these crazy feelings swirling around in our heads.

The stories I share in this book are based on true experiences I've had with many thousands of families during my career as a death care professional—both in and out of the office. While the names and some circumstances have been changed to protect the privacy of my friends and clients, these events really happened. Every one of them.

There's much to learn about what it means to be human from these precious people. They allow us into one of the most intimate parts of their lives. Few experiences are more telling and brutal than when loss of life comes close to us.

Death is the great equalizer. It doesn't care how rich or poor we are, what color our skin is, our age, where in the world we live—or how perfectly healthy our bodies are. It ignores how we are related to the person who died: daughter, son, spouse, brother, sister, friend—even parent or grandparent. Death doesn't care.

Eventually, it comes calling. When it does, we find out what's inside us. This "finding out" comes in short, intense spurts after the loss, as well as more subtle growth which occurs for the rest of our lives. For this axiom is ruthlessly true. Whatever's inside us, when shaken, will most surely come out.

As with everything in life, we're richer if we find ourselves constantly learning from our experiences. But losing a loved one is infinitely more than just a learning opportunity. The realization of our own mortality and of the fragile brevity of life can be a better teacher than all the self-help books in the world. This realization results in a deeper appreciation for living and hopefully, for seeing life as the amazing gift it is.

There are many reasons you were left here on Earth after your loved one died. If you've lost your dad, your mom still needs you. If you've lost both parents, your siblings still need you. If you've lost a spouse, brother, sister or grandparent, someone still needs you.

Even if you've lost a child, there is some cosmic and eternal reason you are still here on Earth. The people who remain still desperately need you. They need you because you matter, you make a difference in the world, you're important.

One more thing. Those "remaining" folks? You also need them.

You need them to be more loving, more compassionate, and more understanding than they've ever been. Although you know in your heart it's impossible for them to fully understand what you're going through, you at least need them to try.

If you allow yourself, as you relate to the precious souls in *Some Perfect Tomorrow*, you may find you're also becoming more loving, compassionate and understanding than you've ever been.

–Craig R. Seaton

CHAPTER 1

The Cry

SHE SAW ME IN THE CEMETERY, coming from a distance. Even though her attention was tightly fixed on his grave, she still saw me. I approached slowly and deliberately from the front so as not to startle her.

As I walked closer, I realized she was likely a new widow in her late 60s or early 70s. A bit plump, drooping shoulders, and a freshly bobbed hairdo from her weekly trip to the beauty shop. The dress was plain. The purse was huge. The spirit crushed.

"Hello," I said, "Is this a loved one you're visiting today?" She didn't move. Except for a clump of hair recently unbobbed by the breeze, she looked like a statue. I stopped a few feet away and clasped my hands. A sign of respect.

You wouldn't think such a common question would merit much more than a nod. Or at best, a subdued yes. Not today.

This was her day. Oh, how she needed this day.

Her head raised slightly. "My husband died three months ago today." The quiver in her voice confessed she was still reeling from the shock. "We were together almost 50 years. We never spent a day apart. Never. Not one day."

She walked around to the head of the grave. Tripping on a small stick, her age-spotted hand reached for something steady. The top of the headstone worked. Its steeled granite felt cool to the touch.

"For fifty years we were always together," she said. "Half a century."

She looked off into the distance and bit her lip. Recalling one of a thousand memories known only to her. Her face changed from nostalgia to anger. A deep breath primed her next words.

"Do you see those sandspurs?" Switching her purse to the other hand, she gestured toward the ground. A bony finger pointed to one of the only sprigs of greenery growing on her husband's grave. "Doesn't anyone take care of this place? There's nothing but dirt. Where's the grass they were going to plant? There was supposed to be fresh sod and there's nothing here but dirt!"

She synchronized the word dirt with her foot kicking a clump of it into the air. It was a hot, dry day. Perfect weather for dirt kicking. The scene reminded me of a major league baseball manager arguing with the home plate umpire. Red Yankee Stadium clay billowing around his feet.

She threw her arms up in annoyance. "Even his headstone is stained! What kind of cemetery is this? I wish I'd never buried him here. I wish...."

The motion caused the huge purse to slip off her shoulder. She bent her elbow, catching it just in time. Walking around to the back side of the headstone she lowered her head. Her eyes searched for something, anything, nothing. She circled back to her original spot at the foot of the grave. There were indentations in the ground where she'd been standing.

I replied softly as her words trailed off. "Ma'am, I'm sorry. I've just begun working here at the cemetery. I'm not sure what I could do, but I…."

As my own words trailed, I made a simple gesture. It was kind of a low shrug that would indicate my innocence for the accused crimes. I lifted my hands ever so slightly from where they'd been hanging and pleaded my case with outturned palms.

That was all she needed. She took my simple gesture as an open invitation. This precious, fragile human being simply melted into my arms. Like a pat of butter on hot toast.

She melted.

With her head buried in my shoulder and her much older arms wrapped around my much younger waist, she let it out.

The cry.

This was the one she'd been holding in since her husband's death. She cried the cry. The initial groan was somehow low and high pitched at the same time. She squeezed those older arms so tightly it nearly knocked the breath out of me. Her whole body was shaking now. It was that involuntary tremble from somewhere deep inside. I'd experienced it before. I knew how it felt.

"I miss him so much," she said. Her words hovered between a whisper and a sigh.

Mixing themselves with the groans almost like a foreign language. "I—miss—him—so—much." The breathy words formed as she inhaled. Her voice was weak. Words turned to moans.

She cried. In the middle of a cemetery. On a normal peaceful sunny day. With a perfect stranger.

It must have lasted only a few minutes. Though it seemed much longer for me—an eternity, even. She didn't need anyone to kill the sandspurs. Fresh sod on his grave was not going to solve this problem. No one needed to fire the cemetery manager. She just needed the cry.

Lifting her head from my shoulder she squared my eyes to hers.

"Do you think someone could at least clean the headstone for me?" A welcomed tone of normalcy returned to her voice. The hint of a smile.

I relaxed my hold around her waist. She stood up straight and stepped back a little. Hug completed. Cry cried. Shifting our weights to get comfortable, we stood apart.

I winged my shoulders back with military resolve. "Yes ma'am. I will have it cleaned first thing tomorrow. I'll also see what we can do about the sod and the sandspurs." She looked away, then back at me.

"Thank you," she said.

The smile was more than hinting now. Her face looked washed out. Cleansed. A byproduct of a good sob. Tear tracks settled in the care lines carved into her cheeks. She wiped her eyes with the back of her hand.

It was one of those rare times in my life. I knew I was exactly where I was supposed to be. Those moments are few. They can't be planned. The stuff real life is made of.

I couldn't wear that suit jacket again until the day I picked it up from the cleaners. Some of her best tears anointed the lapel.

The beauty of life often invades the mystery of death.

There's a lady out there somewhere who still misses her husband. She may not remember an anonymous hug in the middle of a cemetery. Or a stranger in a dark blue suit.

A stranger who will never forget the cry.

Sparks of Life

There's no time limit on grieving, nor is there a set schedule. Some well-meaning folks will tell you there is. They're wrong. Mourning, yes. We can't mourn forever; yet sometimes grief never leaves us. What is important is to recognize the difference between mourning and grief.

If you've lost someone close, you'll most likely go through all the emotions known to humankind. Sadness, anger, bitterness, regret, denial, among many others. These may come at any time, in any order and in any combination. In fact, if you are not experiencing any of these check your pulse. These emotions are normal, even—in some cases—healthy. After all, you are human.

It's not unusual for someone who needs you to fall into your path. You could just as easily fall into theirs. While you certainly shouldn't go looking for these encounters, be silently prepared for them. There's a reason you live on this planet and share its space with others. They need you. You need them.

Some perfect tomorrow does exist. It exists in an imperfect today. A shadowed yesterday. In empathy created every time we peek into another soul. In their struggle. In you.

CHAPTER 2

Grandpas and Angels

"Oh, I'm sorry," Grandpa said. He lowered his head and shrugged his shoulders. "I didn't know there was someone else in here."

"It's okay. I'm just waiting." Was the only reply.

The semiprivate hospital room contained two beds. The one by the window was empty. The other provided comfort for the precious lady with whom Grandpa spent the last 65 years. Sadly, this bed would also be the last place on earth she would be alive.

Only moments after Grandpa peeked around the privacy curtain and saw the "just waiting" man at the window, he turned back to her bedside and again took her hand.

He'd held her hand more times than he could remember. On their first date when his was a little sweaty. At the altar when she looked into his hopeful eyes.

"Of course, I do, sweetie." She'd said in her western Pennsylvania chime. Promising to spend the rest of her life with him. At their 50th wedding anniversary a few years back surrounded by all their children.

Today.

Today, he held it tighter than usual. He watched her chest faintly rise and fall as it did for several days now. He sat like a soldier at her bedside. Rarely surrendering his grip.

Her chest fell and didn't rise again.

In one swift and timeless moment, she was gone.

Grandpa loosened his grip. There's no way of knowing what he was thinking. No way of visualizing what must've been whirling around inside his mind. He just wasn't ready to let her go.

Eventually he did. The muscles in his hand fought hard against the signals from his brain to release his grip. The yearning in his heart to keep holding on to hers. Grandpa stood up and just looked at her face. He knew it better than his own. Somehow, he finally found the strength to look away. He stepped around the curtain and couldn't believe what he saw. The window offered only its daylight, washing the room in pale yellow and white.

The man who was standing there a few seconds ago was gone. He was simply no longer there. There was no way the man could have left the room without passing by. There were other family members outside the door. Surely, they would've seen him.

"Melissa, did you see anyone come out of your Grandma's room just now?" Grandpa asked. He thumbed his earlobe like he always did.

"No sir." Melissa said. She held in a chuckle as she caught herself thumbing her own earlobe. "Rob and I have been sitting right here. We haven't seen anyone." She leaned back in her chair and continued flipping magazine pages. Innocently unaware her grandmother just died.

Grandpa checked the room again. He peeked into the little bathroom, looked around the room once more. He would have noticed the man leaving. Grandpa noticed everything. Yet, this time, he did not.

Nor did anyone else.

In those final moments of life, when death is only a few breaths away, some odd tales are told. You don't have to talk with many people before this kind of story surfaces. These are the events which let us know there's more to living life on Planet Earth than we could ever know. More mystery. More puzzles. More incomprehensible happenings.

In the weeks following, Grandpa talked about the man in the room. "He just looked different. I'm telling you. He was different." His standard reply whenever the subject was raised. "Those last few moments of Grandma's life have swirled around in my head every single day since her passing."

Grandpa closed his eyes. Thumbed his lobe. He remembered the details. Those principal elements in the little scene.

Holding her hand.

Peeking around the curtain.

"I'm just waiting...."

Her last breath.

The empty window.

He knew what he'd seen. He knew the man was real.

It's impossible to live with another person for such a long time and not have this mysterious bond develop. Call it what you will: love, affection, familiarity.

There are those who believe there's nothing more to it than chemical reactions in the brain.

Some things just can't be explained no matter how hard we try.

Grandpa swore until the day he joined Grandma it was an angel who was waiting for her. He told a few of his children. None of them believed him. The only person who did was one of his youngest granddaughters. She had no problem with the story. I guess it depends on your frame of mind. Your perspective.

Sometimes grown-ups can miss what only a child or a grandpa can see.

Sparks of Life

When you lose someone close to you, realize there are mysteries about life and death you just can't explain.

═══

Remember when you were a child and you had that "sense of wonder?" A little slice could be comforting during the unexplainable times.

═══

The connection you have with those close to you goes far beyond a physical and emotional bond. Don't be too quick to discount miracles.

═══

Some perfect tomorrow is a fitting home for the unknown. Not the spooky kind. The laying on your back, gazing at a billion stars kind.

CHAPTER 3

A Child Shall Lead Them

"Mommy, I saw Papa last night." Jeremy's tiny sure voice was serious. "He wanted me to tell you not to worry and he was all right."

"You did Baby?" His mom's eyes moistened. "I think that's really nice, Hon. It must've been a really good dream."

"No, Mommy it wasn't a dream. He was in my room. Papa was standing right there at my bed like he always did when he came upstairs to tell me goodnight." Jeremy looked his mom square in the eye.

Jeremy Munson made up stories like all children do and he could tell some real whoppers. His mom could always tell those tales from something that really happened as he'd have a playful glint in his eye from the first word. Jeremy was a good honest boy and a lousy liar. It was one of his mother's favorite things about him. The glint revealed the joy he felt by sharing his child's fantasy world with her.

The make-believe yarns he usually spun were bizarre. Far-fetched stories of yellow spacemen, wild werewolves (that were actually tamed housecats in real life), and tiny invisible beetle people who ate Jell-O with their feet.

Tonight, as he spoke of seeing his grandfather, the glint in Jeremy's eye was absent.

"I really saw him, Mommy. Papa was standing right there." He pointed to the spot at the end of his bed where Dawn Munson's dad stood every night when he came to tuck Jeremy into bed. He'd stand in the spot, bend over to give him a kiss on the forehead and then pull up the covers to Jeremy's shoulders. Papa would always say the same thing.

"Night-night, Buddy. Sleep tight. Don't let the bed bugs bite. If they do, bite 'em back!"

Jeremy's papa died six months ago. After a brief fight with cancer, he'd lost the battle. He went to sleep one night and didn't wake up. Dawn was a daddy's girl. She'd been so her whole life. Just because she was 42 now didn't change that one bit.

Being a daddy's girl meant when he died it left her more than just half-orphaned. Jeremy missed him too, but a grandparent dying to a seven-year-old is sometimes more like a fairy tale than a real event. "Papa is in Heaven." This was his understanding. To Jeremy it was like his grandfather was on vacation somewhere for a very long time.

Dawn missed her dad every moment of every minute of every hour of every day. The funeral was hard. The burial was harder. The memories though, were the hardest of all. Yes, she had to get on with life. No one needed to tell her that. She had a job and a family to take care of.

Now, threaded through her daily routine were those memories. The deep, unresolvable knowing her dad was gone. Jeremy's papa would never return from this vacation.

Not this one.

Sometimes adults try to make the death of a loved one something we can manage. It's like it needs to somehow fit in with other events in our lives so we can mark it on our calendars. Soccer game, mortgage due date, Carol and Fred's wedding, company picnic, oil change and tire rotation. Dad's death.

The problem is death doesn't fit in anywhere. It's a nagging entity in the back of our minds which surfaces at the oddest times. We don't seem to be able to control and compartmentalize it as we do those other things. It's easy to deal with simple life stuff: school, work, driving, watching a movie, getting dressed in the morning or cooking a meal.

Losing someone you've loved with all your heart belongs on an entirely different planet.

"Jeremy," His mom bent over and cupped her hands around his chubby little cheeks. "I miss Papa too. Sometimes I wish I could see him again. He loved you so much, you know."

Dawn's eyes were more than moist now. The tears were falling everywhere. Her mind raced through four decades of having her father in her life and all that meant to her now. She stood up straight and closed her eyes hard. Tears flowed down wrinkled paths, framing her face in wet lines. Her expression softened as the memories rushed in.

In an instant she was being pushed on the old tire swing. Sitting on his lap at the ballgame. Licking her hand (and his) as the ice cream dripped over their cones on a hot Georgia summer day. Walking down the aisle at church when he gave her away. Holding his hand for hours in the hospital when he didn't even know who she was. God she missed him.

"I'd like to see him again Jeremy," she said.

The memories faded as quickly as they came. Then something amazing happened.

Jeremy stood on his tip toes. His little hands reached up, cupped his mother's cheeks and pulled her face down close to his. With his tiny sure voice, which was honest, he looked into her eyes.

"You can see him, Mommy. You just have to become a little girl again," he said.

Some things are hard to understand. The precious heart and unpolluted mind of a child is impossible to explain. I hope we never do.

Sparks of Life

Child-like faith believes things grown-ups dismiss as dreams or chemical reactions. If you've lost this kind of faith, spend everything you must to get it back. Everything.

Lost loved ones imprinted their very souls onto ours when they were alive. We are connected in ways we may never understand. While it's hard and hurts deeply, the connection can enrich your life. Let it.

When life after a loss seems futile and the future looks bleak, go buy yourself an ice cream cone and let its melting fluids drip down your hand on a summer day. When no one's looking, skip for a few steps on your way out of the dollar store (where you just bought some Crayons and a coloring book). You'll find the child inside is still very much alive. He is just waiting to cup your cheeks, pull your face down, and innocently whisper love in your grown-up ear.

Some perfect tomorrow holds on to pleasant memories as if they were life itself. Sometimes they can be.

CHAPTER 4

A Laughable Funeral

"LAUGHTER AT A FUNERAL is proof death is not as bad as it seems."

It's one of my original quotes. You're free to use it. I hope it proves true at your funeral—I hope the event is a very, very long time off.

Nick Ward is a tonic. No matter how bad you feel, how lousy of a day you've had, or even how you ended up in a stuffy funeral home chapel for the memorial service of a friend. Nick Ward has a way of making you feel like everything is going to be all right.

When Nick was chosen to speak at Jack Norse's funeral service, I knew it was going to be a memorable day. In years past, Nick and I worked with Jack. Jack was known to have one of the most infectious smiles around. He would always have a cup of coffee in his hand. Always. And the smile was his trademark.

Nick and I were in the Navy together. Jack, who retired from the Navy after 20 years, now worked in civil service as a Flight Simulator Operator in Jacksonville, Florida. Nick worked directly with Jack and even though I was in a different department, I'd see them several times throughout the day.

Jack and his wife Lola were two of the sweetest people you'd ever want to meet. They loved each other deeply and spent their lives together raising children and, like many today, raising a few grandchildren as well.

The cancer took them all completely by surprise. Its insidious and rapid spread took Jack's life. At the young age of 77, he left his wife and family to live out the rest of their lives without him. He didn't take everything with him. He left them with thousands of good memories to embrace and cherish for the rest of their lives.

Even though Jack Norse lived on his humble Navy pension and underpaid civil service salary, he was one of the wealthiest men I've ever known. Jack's wealth had nothing to do with his bank account or how well he managed his money. It was the good memories he deposited in the hearts of his family and friends. Jack had true wealth. This wealth lived on even after he died.

The chapel was quickly filling as the families made their way in. A group of four, a couple, a single guy. They all filed in. Jack's family was sitting in the front row. As with most funerals, the mood was somber and hushed tones were the volume of the day. The music played softly as the two o'clock starting time approached. Seats were taken. Music stopped. Voices muted. A few deep breaths completed the introduction.

Nick Ward made his way past the casket and stepped up to the podium directly behind it. "Hi, my name's Nick." He began Jack's funeral service the same way he'd started thousands of conversations over the years. Nick Ward never met a stranger.

"I don't have to tell you why we're all here today. We all know Jack's body is there right in front of me." He pointed down to the open casket.

The lower part of the burnished silver casket was draped in red, white and blue. An honorable gift from the grateful nation Jack served for so many years.

"But, if we concentrate on the casket, we're missing the point," he continued. Nick flashed his famous smile. It lit up the room like it always did. Those pearly whites didn't care this was a funeral home chapel.

Nick scanned the front row and locked eyes with Jack's widow. "I'm pretty sure he wouldn't want us to do that anyway. Knowing Jack, I think he would want us to take some time and think about how he lived while he was with us."

He choked back a tear and swallowed hard as he remembered his good friend.

"There are many things I could say. Lots of Bible verses I could read. Lots of yarns I could spin," he said.

Then, to my surprise, he folded and put away whatever papers he'd brought to the podium as if finishing his speech after a mere 30 seconds of prologue. Most funeral preachers would've had 20 to 30 minutes of material still ahead. Not Nick. He had an agenda, and it was near-magical.

"Since most of the people Jack loved are right here in this room, I think it would be most fitting if it were those people who 'preached' his funeral."

Nick looked around the room. A few attendees squirmed in their seats, visibly surprised by the absence of decorum found at most memorial services and wondering what would happen next.

"Who's got a story or memory they'd like to share with us?"

Silence. Whoosh. A few pins made their way to the floor and were heard making their tiny dropping-pin sounds.

A thin, aging man slowly stood about halfway up the aisle. "I'd like to say something," he began. He was a bit stiff and hesitant. "What I remember most about Jack was back when we were young bucks in the Navy together," he said. He mounted his hands on his hips. His voice was raspy. He cleared his throat a few times. His wife handed him a bottle of water.

"We got into our fair share of trouble back then." He twisted at the waist from side to side as he spoke. Trying to target the whole room. "Back in '67 we were on shore leave in Singapore." His Texas accent rang across the room. "Well, Jack and I were on shore patrol, and…"

He spent the next three or four minutes weaving a vivid tale of young sailors in distant exotic lands. He was a seasoned storyteller and it showed as he bathed in the pleasure of the crowd's reactions.

It began with a light chuckle from somewhere in the back of the room, then a subdued laugh or two in the front. By the time he was near the end of the memory, the room filled with a warmth found only in genuine laughter. Laughter at a funeral service? Yes. It was one of the most beautiful things I've ever witnessed.

Over the next half hour, one by one, people stood and shared memories of how Jack touched their lives. Some were heartfelt, some were tearful, but most were glad, lighthearted tales of how this man enriched their lives in some small way.

As the laugher died down, Jack's brother stood up.

"Most of you know I'm Jack's baby brother." His voice broke as the room quieted. "He loved woodworking. Jack could make anything from wood. Many of you know that."

Heads turned in the crowd. Nodding at each other. Certifying Jack's woodworking legacy.

"Well, I love woodworking too. Jack taught me everything I…" He couldn't make it through the thought. He tried a few more words. No luck. Only high-pitched unintelligible sounds. His wife stood and put a comforting hand on his shoulder. He sat down.

A few of the stories commanded hearty laughter. Shared laughter usually reserved for an evening in the company of a talented stand-up comic or shared with friends you grew up with (the ones who know stuff about you nobody else would ever believe).

We all laughed 'til we cried, cried 'til we caught our breath. Then did it all over again. Jack Norse was a loved man who'd spent his entire life infecting other people with his smile and simple, genuine personality. Now, at the end of Jack's life, the infection was reaping great rewards in this very room.

Nick stood still. He spoke not another word. Read no Bible verses. Delivered no prepared sermon. The closest he came to a "traditional" funeral service was to dismiss the gathering with a brief prayer of thanks after everyone finished sharing.

I looked over at Lola, Jack's widow. Widows and widowers are really the centerpiece of most funeral services, not the dearly departed. Their families and friends take great care to see they are comforted. After all, she was the closest person in the whole world to Jack.

Lola had the biggest and brightest grin on her face. Her husband was dead. She'd never see him on Earth again, and she was smiling.

A laughable funeral. A smiling widow. Death and life. Lots of life.

Sparks of Life

There's a reason we've been given the Gift of Memory. Yes, memories can be painful, even debilitating. Those are the ones we need to file away forever. There are good ones too. Those are the ones which sustain us.

When you find laughter again, it's not disrespectful to the one you've lost. It's really a sign of hope, of goodness—of life itself.

If we're brutally honest with ourselves, would the one we've lost want us crying?

Some perfect tomorrow is embodied in the lives of people who affect others in a positive way. Life is hard. Really hard. We know it is. Positive people can help make it softer. Loving people can help make it bearable. Bearable softness. Jack Norse.

CHAPTER 5

Get Over It?

"**D**ON'T YOU THINK IT'S TIME YOU JUST GOT OVER IT? I mean, she died almost three years ago and you're acting like it just happened yesterday."

Heather's words hung over Rose Marie's head like one of those Sunday comics word balloons. This particular balloon was made of lead.

Try as she may to just "get over it" (whatever that looked like) it just wasn't happening. At least not as fast as all her well-meaning friends and family told her it should be. Should. An interesting word. Should seemed to work so well for everyone else.

Before the breath had finished forming her friend's words, Rose Marie Rodriguez's mind was already back sitting at her mother's bedside three years ago.

Juanita Rodriguez, the one who'd given her birth. The one who'd been her constant companion through life. Who'd sacrificed so much to give her everything she didn't have when she was a little girl. Her mom was in a hospice room, bravely succumbing to a four-year fight with breast cancer.

Rose Marie's mother, who'd now been gone an eternity, three years, was at once a living, breathing memory. Alive again in seconds within her mind.

If you've ever lost someone close to you there's literally no difference between your heart and theirs. You know exactly how Rose Marie was feeling. This closeness is especially true with mothers and daughters. There is the natural connection a mother has with her children. After all she nurtured them inside her own body for months.

With women, there's a mystical affinity rarely found in men. It's certainly emotional, but it goes beyond mere emotion. Maybe it's spiritual or even physical.

Rose Marie felt that spiritual connection this moment. It swirled around her mind and gushed in waves over her body. She tussled with memories she'd tried to suppress. Losing her mom was hard. The hardest thing she'd ever done. Ever. The thoughts were magnified as she dwelled on the fact Juanita Rodriguez barely had a chance to be a grandmother. Before the cancer stole her away. Forty-five was too young to die.

Fighting hard to regain control over her thoughts, she finally mustered the strength to respond to her friend's comment.

"I know I need to get over it, Heather. At least I think I know I do. Every time I feel I've made a step toward healing I take two back. Sometimes I walk back a whole mile of steps."

The tears wouldn't stay back any longer. Rose Marie wept. Her hands covered her face.

"I feel like I just betrayed my mother again by even admitting I was 'healing.' I know Mother wouldn't want me to mourn for the rest of my life."

Rose Marie felt uncomfortable saying those words out loud. There was some strange self-sustaining guilt she carried with her. Anytime she felt herself relaxing and enjoying the moment, the guilt would surface and rob her joy.

"It's almost like missing my mother every waking moment is my own cross to bear."

She relaxed her posture. She didn't realize how tense she'd become talking about it. Heather sensed her ease and took a deep breath.

"Rose Marie, you know I love you like my own sister and I would never do anything to hurt you," Heather said. "It's just I hate to see you so sad all the time. I want you to start living again that's all. That's what I meant."

Rose Marie smiled through the tears. She embraced her good friend with one of those famous Rodriguez hugs. The kind that will squeeze the air from your lungs if it catches you between breaths.

"Thank you, Heather. I feel like you're the only friend I have." She held her as she spoke. Clasped her fingers in the small of her back. Two friends. Swaying.

"Mom and I were so close. No one could ever understand me like she did. You are such a faithful friend. You've always been there for me. Thank you. You're my angel."

Heather was crying now. Tears everywhere. Rose Marie kissed her on the cheek.

"It's all right honey." She patted Heather's back. Rubbing her shoulders. Even in her grief Rose Marie Rodriguez was comforting another.

The heaviness started to lift after Heather showed up on the scene. Rose Marie thought long and hard about her grief, her mom and her lifelong friend. It only took a second to inventory the blessings she had in her life. Two beautiful children, a husband who was a good provider, her family's health, good friends. The list went on. The list kept her going when she felt like giving up.

"You know, Heather, counting your blessings sometimes sounds so trite. So, cliché." Rose Marie held her hand to her heart. Thumping her palm on her chest in rhythm with her words.

"I think there's something to it. Something happens in me when I concentrate on the positives in my life." Her eyes narrowed like she was peeking out window blinds on a sunny day. Her voice went higher.

"Instead of those nagging negatives that pin me down."

Her voice cracked. She forced the final words out. Her face looked shades lighter. The glow returned to her eyes.

"I'm grateful. I really am."

Rose Marie smiled and got in one last hug. The good friends walked down the steep driveway. Said their goodbyes for the ninth time. Heather got in her car and drove off. Rose Marie watched until she was out of sight.

Something deep inside Rose Marie began to stir. It started a little like butterflies in her stomach and then grew into an almost tangible warmth. She'd had this feeling before. Every time it left her almost breathless. She knew it was much more than a feeling though. Much more than chemicals and enzymes in her brain. It was hope. It felt good.

This time, it felt more than good. It felt final. She'd nailed something to that cross of hers she'd carried for the last three years. Rose Marie tried to see it in her mind's eye. She found herself trying to focus as if it were visible. By this time the warmth made its way from her belly and enveloped her entire self. She was warm. She was peaceful. She was happy.

It was this very moment, the precious and fleeting moment, she realized she missed her mom like crazy, and it was okay.

Sparks of Life

Few things in life can be as healing as the moment grieving turns to joy. Embrace these moments. Realize more will come.

There is no time limit on grief. Many books address the subject. None should propose a deadline. No words, written or spoken, can tell you when your grief will change. But when it changes (and it will) you'll know yourself better. You'll be richer for the experience.

Did you recognize Heather? If you don't have a Heather in your life, drop this book at once and go find yourself one. Your Heather may not be a lifelong friend. There are many people out there waiting to listen to you and love you just like you are. Don't make them wait too long.

Some perfect tomorrow is a black hole for debilitating guilt. It simply cannot exist there. Guilt for wrong against another? Yes. Good guilt to have. Leads us to make things right with self. With others. The world. Guilt for feelings of regret and what could have been? No way. There is too much life to do. Too much you to be.

CHAPTER 6

Michelangelo's Pieta

"HE DIED IN MY ARMS, YOU KNOW. I was holding him just like this." She cradled her arm as one would a baby. "He'd been sick for so long. I knew God wanted to ease his pain."

Mrs. Jensen was tired. You could see it. Her face was care-worn, stained with years of being strong for her family. Taking care of George Jensen was her life for a very long time.

"It's been two months now and I still haven't cried. Everyone says I'm strong. I'm so tired of being strong," she said under her breath. Her eyes left mine and found the floor. "I've taken care of him for 65 years." She looked back up at me. Her eyes were misty. Spread fingers brushed back a curl of grey and auburn hair.

Sixty-five years. I haven't even been alive for 65 years.

This was one of those days. When you lose someone, there are certain days which are harder than others. Sometimes it's a birthday, an anniversary or even something invisible to others in your life—like the day you always celebrated, just the two of you.

When cemetery interment is chosen as the final disposition, there remains the difficult task of designing a memorial or headstone to mark the grave.

Aside from my work as a funeral planner, I am also a memorialist (monument designer). Helping a family with their headstone is one of the most precious and favorite parts of my job. There's just something about having a part in carving someone's legacy into solid granite or casting it into bronze which stamps a note of permanence onto one's work. This is something which will be here long after we're gone.

Today was Mrs. Jensen's appointment with me to design her husband's monument. Today, she would choose how future generations remembered her husband—at least when they stood at his grave. Consider the weight of this kind of decision for a moment. In modern 21st Century life, few of us take much thought of future generations, ours, or anyone else's.

"Mrs. Jensen let me ask you something," I started the conversation. "After we're all gone—you, me, even your children, when people stand at George's grave, what do you want them to know about him?"

It was a question I asked every family. It helps paint a perpetual picture of the importance, and the lasting result of the decisions we'll make during the design process. It brings "next month" closer to, "a hundred years from now."

After giving me a long, purposeful look, she cocked her head and gazed distantly as if scrolling through memories known only to her and George.

"You know," she almost whispered, "remember I told you he died in my arms?"

I nodded.

"Well, I saw a photo of an old sculpture the other day which reminded me of that moment. I'm not very religious as far as church-going and all that stuff, but this really affected me."

I instantly knew she was talking about Michelangelo's Pieta, but I let her continue, not wanting to spoil her train of thought with my details.

"It was the Virgin Mary. She was holding Jesus in her lap after they'd taken him down from the cross. She had the most solemn expression on her face—kind of like she wasn't really sad anymore, just…"

Mrs. Jensen's head turned the other way to gather her thoughts. You could tell she was trying to find just the right words.

"…like she was accepting his death."

The words barely left her lips when I saw the tears of reality welling up inside her. She closed her eyes and tried to hold them back, but they wouldn't be tamed. These were tears she'd been holding in for quite some time, maybe years. They needed out. They needed out now.

It was one of the most cleansing cries I'd ever seen. I let her fully embrace it as I remained silent and still. She gathered herself together and came back from the place the tears had taken her. I knew it was purposed and needed. She took a deep breath.

"I don't think I'd ever related to Mary in this specific way until I saw the photo of the Pieta."

Then she leveled me with her next words.

"The look on her face was exactly how I felt when I was holding George in those last moments of his life. I never realized until just a moment ago. God, I miss him so much." She bit both lips for a moment before finishing her sentence. "But I am so glad he's not suffering anymore."

I've said it before, one thing I constantly pray is I never get used to what I do. I knew what she would say next.

"I'd like to somehow incorporate Michelangelo's Pieta into George's monument," she said. "I feel a connection to Mary in some small way and, like you said, I want people to know this when they stand at his grave."

The 21st century of Northeast Florida and the 15th century of Western Italy are separated by thousands of miles and hundreds of years. On this day, a sweet lady was affected half a millennium after an artist's depiction of something which happened 1500 years before he, Michelangelo, was even born.

It made a difference. It really does matter how we choose to be remembered. When I finally got in my car for the drive home, I knew it was a good day.

Sparks of Life

Don't let anyone (including yourself) tell you that you'll ever "get over" the one you lost. Do everything in your power to ensure their memories live on.

———

Even though cremation is gaining popularity, it doesn't mean you can't somehow memorialize your loved one so your descendants can share some of what your life together meant to you.

———

Embracing the fact people have gone to great lengths to ensure their memories last, do something which makes you feel like you've "left your mark." (The Pyramids aren't just for Pharaohs.)

———

Some perfect tomorrow is not fearful of yesterday. It welcomes it. Monuments are erected in town squares to help us remember. Whether actual physical structures or shared memories, memorials are vital for our wellbeing. They remind us who we are. You create a lasting "mental monument" every time you think of good memories. Pass them on.

CHAPTER 7

It's Not Your Fault

THE FIRST THING I NOTICED was the handgun strapped to his side. As he came closer, I glanced between the gun and his face. My eyes scanned a dozen other devices strapped to his belt. Most I didn't recognize.

Dark green uniform. Combat-style boots. Radio microphone clipped to his collar. Gold star above his left shirt pocket. Handcuffs tucked in the back of his belt. Friendly smile.

Friendly smile?

Yes, friendly smile. It's always better to have a deputy sheriff stop you when you're walking into your favorite breakfast haunt than approach your car from behind while a million sparkles of light paint the landscape blue.

The haunt was Country Cabin Restaurant, the best breakfast spot in town at the time. The deputy was Sergeant Jim Cramer, an old friend of mine. Fortunately, he was stopping me to say, "good morning" and swap some banter instead of telling me I was "in a heap of trouble, boy." We both sat down at our table and ordered coffee.

I would venture most everyone who knows I'm in the funeral business feels compelled from time to time to swap a tale about their experiences with death. This reflexive compulsion we possess to share our personal stories with other folks is one of the greatest things which make us human.

We air our aches and pains to folks in the medical field. We talk plants with the lady down the way who owns the nursery. Camaraderie. Common ground. So, having my friends and acquaintances tell me about their experiences with death is expected. I don't mind listening.

After some small talk, I knew he was aching to open up about how he was really doing.

"My partner was standing right beside me when he was shot," Jim said. He broke into this story seamlessly from whatever it was we were talking about 12 seconds ago. "I saw the muzzle flash and heard the thud as the bullet hit him. He was down in a split second."

I listened as he relived this drug bust which took the life of his fellow officer and wounded another. I could tell it wounded Jim too. His scars were different. This was the first time we talked privately since the incident.

"The low-life who operated the meth lab we were raiding fired the fatal shot." He clenched his teeth and tightened his grip on the coffee cup handle. "One of my other buddies was hit in the brachial artery of his right arm. He simply switched his revolver to his other hand. Put his fingers over the wound and continued shooting."

Jim's face softened as his jaw relaxed. A cleansing breath powered his next words.

"His was one of many shots which took the meth guy out. Not until we'd lost one of the force's best—all because of some dirt-bag's warped idea not going to jail was worth taking the life of a police officer." His eyes were moist now. The heart behind the badge. "My partner left behind a wife and two toddlers."

My friend is not usually an outwardly tender-hearted person. I don't think any first responder can be—at least not while in the line of duty. Today I peeked inside his soul. He'd loved his partner and it still hurt him every day he was gone.

"It reminded me of a war scene," he said. "Not different than walking beside your buddy on the battlefield one minute, and then he's gone the next. No difference at all."

Jim's big hands tried hard to find something to do. He fidgeted with the coffee cup. Rolled his wedding ring in his thumb. Twisted a napkin. He looked out the window at his patrol car.

It's never easy when someone dies. Many would say when a terrible illness like cancer, or Lou Gehrig's disease, or AIDS was bravely battled, it's almost a blessing in disguise when they finally succumb to the inevitable. No one wants to see a person they love suffer.

Not so with sudden deaths like this murder of a police officer, or an automobile crash, a drive-by shooting or a tragic drowning. These events rip our hearts from our chests and send us reeling in disbelief. How many times have we heard things like this? "Wow, I just talked to him on the phone Friday." Or, "I knew something didn't seem right that day." Or, "She was just at my house last night."

My friend would've given anything to have the moment back—just before the fatal shot came.

"I've relived it more times than I can remember," he said. He tried to hide wiping a tear then looked back at me. "There are times at night when it plays over and over in my mind and no matter what; I just can't turn it off."

He picked up his coffee cup which hadn't left the table until now. He took a long sip. It seemed to help.

"Jim," I said, "It's natural to blame ourselves when things like this happen. There's nothing I can say to you to make those memories go away."

Jim lowered his head in agreement and stared down at the table.

"But, my friend, if I could say just one thing, it would have to be it wasn't your fault, Jim."

His eyes were getting wetter. You could tell it was making him uncomfortable. He was on duty and in full uniform. His sense of disciplined police duty gave way, if only for a moment, to his sense of being human.

I wanted to reach across the table and give him a hug, but I decided a purposeful pat on his folded hands would be best for now. He glanced at me with a silent thank you. With a dim smile, he stood up, leaving me to finish a freshly poured cup of coffee. I wondered what this 12-hour shift would bring for Jim.

We must all face the certainty that this life—which we so often take for granted—is much more fragile and fleeting than we know.

When this kind of loss slaps us in the face, we find ourselves saying things like, "If I'd just done 'this' or if I'd not done 'that' they would still be alive today."

If he could, I'm sure Jim's partner would say, "There was nothing you could've done, my friend. Don't beat yourself up for something you'll never be able to reconcile. It's not your fault."

It's not your fault.

Sparks of Life

If you've lost someone suddenly, it may not seem real they're gone. Maybe not for a very long time, if ever.

Let the memories come and linger for a while. The painful ones, the fuzzy ones. The joyful ones. You'll find healing there somewhere.

It's not your fault. Realizing this may be the most important thing you can do. It's not your fault.

Some perfect tomorrow has grace for every shame we carry. Grief shapes itself in miraculous ways when echoed with grace. It will shape you. Listen for the echo.

CHAPTER 8

I Love Parking Lots

WHEN SOMEONE DIES, it changes us somehow. Changes the way we act, the way we speak, the way we think. For a little while anyway.

It was a humid Florida evening and the funeral chapel was filling with well-wishers coming to pay their respects. Some were standing around quietly. Some sat in an available chair or pew. Others talked in hushed tones. A few shared a common story. Some looked sad, others scared. The immediate family sat in the front few rows greeting folks as they came by.

If you've ever been to an open-casket funeral, you may have noticed people act different when they're in the presence of a formerly living human, surrounded by currently living humans. Somehow it doesn't feel natural. Yet death is quite natural. How it affects us is natural. We all react differently. We are human.

This gathering was held the night before the funeral service was to be held at a church. In a traditional American funeral service, it's called the Viewing, the Visitation, or the Wake. In some areas of the country it's known as Calling Hours.

For a traditional open-casket funeral service, this is the time when family and friends experience the initial brunt of seeing their loved one lying in state. Some folks say seeing a person lying dead in a long wooden or metal box is morbid. They would never wish this for anyone. Others consider the open casket normal. It "doesn't really seem like a funeral" if there's no open casket.

To me, it's quite normal since I'd seen it a few hundred times a year for a few decades. On a personal level, I've also witnessed my very own parents, grandparents, and almost every one of my aunts and uncles in one of those long boxes. Yes, it's quite normal to me. Morbid or not, it provides comfort for many.

I scanned the room and a few folks caught my eye. There was this one man who'd been standing off by himself most of the evening. I'd noticed him earlier. He'd kept his distance from the casket and was not overly friendly with anyone. He'd glance away when most people walked by and only made eye contact with a few. I thought he was a distant friend or one of those eccentric uncles who always flies in from out of town. You know the one who's lived in a mountain cabin in northwestern Canada all his life. The one whom all the others think is a little strange.

Turns out he was one of the deceased's sons. Not even the son who may have spent his summers with Canadian Uncle. He was a close son, geographically at least. He lived in the same town. On the same street.

Standing over by the casket was the daughter who helped her mom with the funeral arrangements when her dad died suddenly three days ago. She was a bright, gregarious lady who obviously knew everyone. She wore a light-yellow skirt and a burnt orange top. Given her personality, she would have looked out of place in the traditional black.

While keeping a handkerchief at ready, she talked, listened, even laughed with a few people as they spoke of her dad. They spun yarns from their memories of him when he was young. Most of which were likely exaggerated for a good punch line.

I stood in the rear of the chapel, away from the family but watching for any need: an empty tissue box, a late-arriving floral arrangement, a subtle glance from his widow meaning, "I need you."

I was intrigued by these siblings and how different they were. It would be easy to make a judgment about them. How they were getting through this part of the funeral ritual in very different ways.

Is he just sad? Does she just not care? Was he adopted? Was she just hiding her true feelings by being the life of the party? You know the thoughts. We all have them.

Turns out, I wouldn't look good in one of those long black flowing robes, seated behind one of those towering oaken "benches" and handing down fair and impartial rulings. I wouldn't make a good judge. None of my judgments were correct.

The next day, after the funeral, I witnessed one of the truly beautiful things loss can do to a family. I later learned Brother and Sister hadn't spoken in years. She was the high-society lady. He was the introverted loner. She knew everyone in town. He knew a few. She drove a luxury SUV. He didn't even have a driver's license. She couldn't stand his ways. He hated hers. Death has a way of equalizing great gaps. It bridges economic and social chasms like no other event in life.

There were only a few cars left in the parking lot when I noticed the two of them talking. I'd not seen them exchange even a single word until now. Then, the beauty happened. He opened his arms, she hers. They embraced.

Brother and Sister held each other for what seemed like a very long time. I could even see them gently shaking, quivering—like someone will do when they're sobbing deeply. I'm not sure what was said between them before and after this encounter, but whatever it was, it was healing. It was beautiful.

I wondered why they'd waited until their dad died to fix whatever was broken between them. I wondered why this beautiful healing didn't come years ago.

I walked back into the funeral home with a smile on my face and a warmth in my heart.

When someone dies, it changes us somehow.

Sparks of Life

An adage from the 1960s and 70s was, "Today is the first day of the rest of your life." There's more truth in this statement than we know. Truth which says any relationship can be bettered. Not all, but the ones that matter.

Few of us can say we have a perfect connection with everyone in our lives. Be honest with yourself. Inventory those relationships which could use some shoring up.

You can't wait until someone dies before you "say what you've always wanted to say" to them. You do a disservice to them, yourself and your relationship. Don't wait.

Some perfect tomorrow never promises an easy road. It hopes for fewer rocks along the way. Hopes for a day when the rocks are cleared. All the rocks. When the road becomes a vibrant stream. Running clear and true. Revealing a better us.

CHAPTER 9

Eleanor Rigby's Husband

"YOU SEE THE CHAIR IN THE CORNER? He died right there. He loved that old chair." She paused. "The last place on Earth he was alive." Her eyes began to mist. She glanced down at the chair. Looking for him. "He'd sit there for hours and read, do a crossword or just look out at the lake."

I'd dropped by Mrs. Rigby's house on my way home from the office. After a few months, she was finally ready to think about what type of headstone she wanted for his grave. Although the reason for my visit was to design her husband's monument, I soon learned my true purpose was more substantial.

"I still can't believe he's gone," she said. "I find myself staring at the old chair sometimes for hours. I still see him sitting in it. Not in a spooky, ghostly way. His essence, his spirit, his presence. He's there." She stared out the window as she spoke as if dredging up a distant memory. She had lines on her face from years of caring. A broken heart from years of loving. Mrs. Rigby talked a long time about the details of her husband's heart attack.

"I feel so alone now." She blinked a few times. A nervous twitch tickled the corner of her mouth. "It helps me when I reminisce. Clears my mind." She released a deep sigh and looked drained. The drain seemed good and the sigh cleansing. Maybe even prescribed.

I sat quietly. Listening intently to her heartfelt words.

"Mrs. Rigby," I said, "I'm in no hurry. If we never get to the business at hand it will be okay. You take as long as you need."

She took a few long breaths. Relaxed. For a moment.

"My husband's death would be difficult enough. Losing my son six weeks later has left me beyond numb," she said. Her face confirmed her words. She peered into nowhere. Eyes frozen. Deep in thought. "I'm not sure how I'm supposed to feel. How I should deal with it. I never thought I'd have to bury the two most important men in my life."

Without warning, she dove headfirst into the harrowing circumstances of the death of her youngest son.

"I think my son's death affected me in a whole other way. No parent should ever bury a child. It goes against everything civilized human beings know to be good and true and right." She wringed her hands and looked around for something to fidget with. A blue rubber coated paper clip worked. Her eyebrows narrowed. She sucked her lips between her teeth. The next words hurt.

"My son was tragically killed in a freak accident. He'd just that morning kissed me on the cheek." Her voice was breaking now. She waited for the emotion to pass. It took a minute.

"His final farewell was his trademark salutation, 'See you in a few minutes, Mom.'" Mrs. Rigby wept. Her deep pain flowed from her wounded heart. Her body shook. Moans turned to whimpers. She calmed herself enough to finish her thought.

"My son told me the same thing since he was old enough to spend the night at a friend's house. He never left without saying…" She held her breath. "…without saying, 'see you in a few minutes.'" She exhaled. Grateful to finally get those words out. Her face relaxed. She found a tissue in her purse. "I never thought it would be the last time I would ever see him." She grew silent. Exhausted from telling the stories yet another time.

If we're honest, we all have this sense in differing degrees. A subtle fear of the last goodbye. We subdue it, suppress it. Stuff it into the "Things That Can Never Happen To Me" storage bin. Way down in the bottom of our thought locker. It still exists.

For many it's more than a nagging thought. You've been through it personally. Whether recently or many years ago, you still remember storing this impossible thought in a thinly lined storage bin.

I don't think Mrs. Rigby needed a headstone for her husband today. She just needed a friend.

Sparks of Life

The String Theory imagines everything in the Universe is connected. You don't need to be a physicist to know humans share a unique connection with other humans. Especially when they share some common event. It may be one of the best things about being human.

Just like this story, someone will cross your path. They will do so for a different reason than you thought. Don't be alarmed since that person won't know either. The true beauty of encounters like these lies in both party's sincere ignorance of the Big Picture happening right under their noses. People loving people when they least expect it.

Even though we all do, it's rarely beneficial to compare what you're going through with someone else's experience. Every loss hurts everyone differently. What can help is knowing there is always something going on deeper than can be seen at the surface. In you and in the people and circumstances you come across each day. It's what makes empathy work both ways.

Some perfect tomorrow wonderfully materializes when empathy prevails. Compassionate understanding brightens the soul. Lightens the step. A little. Some days, a little is all it takes.

CHAPTER 10

The Final Doctor's Appointment

THE VERY FIRST DEATH I EVER WITNESSED could've been a textbook version of Jack Kevorkian's physician-assisted suicide.

You'd think someone in the funeral profession was well-acquainted with death. I am. My professional perspective of death and its effects on life is always post-mortem. Often, I meet with a family who is facing the reality that death is within months, weeks, or even days. Prearranging for a death or helping a family after they've experienced one is an entirely different circumstance from actually being an onlooker when the last breath of life is exhaled from a body. Different indeed.

He was ill for a short time. The cancer went virtually undetected until the last few months of his life. No one deserves to die before their time. We all hope "our time" is as far away as possible. But this guy was not one to let a little thing like dying stop him from living. Right up until a day or two before he left this earth, he was fairly active. He was as active as one can be with millions of malignant cells roaming inside his body. Killing everything they sink their teeth into.

On a normal day, he'd be up early before anyone in the house was even out of bed. He'd grab a quick bite of breakfast and head outside. Inside is a nice place to be and we all need a roof over our heads—but the Outdoors was like a tonic to him. It was as if he belonged there and so he spent most of his waking hours outside.

A walk in the woods, a stroll down the street, exploration of a new site, or just sitting in the back yard enjoying the sunshine and a cool breeze was his best day. It was the perfect day.

If you're like that, it must be even harder when an illness like cancer robs you of your very life-force; whatever it is you do which makes you feel very much alive. Being restricted indoors was a virtual prison in those final days. I think if we could have put a bed in the backyard, he'd been more at ease while he was dying. I considered it a few times.

You see, this death was in my own family. The dynamic changes again.

I'm a professional "death guy" who deals with death every single working day. Often right before it, but most of the time right after it. Now for the very first time I would actually witness it happening. It would happen to one of my very own.

My family. The precious ones I shared my life with day in and day out. It would go down in our family's history as one of the hardest things we've ever done. Ever.

We knew today was going to be the day. We all dreaded this day even though we knew deep within us it was bound to come. When a terminal illness touches your family, a certain hidden camaraderie, even in healthy families like ours, always seems to mysteriously pull people together. I've always marveled at this phenomenon. It happens in triumphs as well as tragedies. There is just something in the human spirit ignited when we acutely need each other more than we do in normal everyday life.

He'd been to the doctor many times throughout his life, but always for a routine checkup, a shot, or to get a prescription refilled. Today's appointment was his final. He wouldn't come back alive from this one.

He was so weak we had to carry him in. We signed some papers and were escorted into one of the examination rooms. The nurse made sure he was comfortable. Then made sure we were comfortable as well.

Through this whole ordeal, he never uttered a single word. Aside from occasional moans caused by his body being in pain, he was very quiet, almost dignified. He knew.

The doctor came in after a few minutes and prepared us for what was to happen. You could tell she was trained in more than just medical science. She had a caring heart and was one of those people who were truly right where they should be. Taking care of sick patients and helping them live. Today she would care for this one by helping him die.

He was laid on the table and a mask placed over his face. A gas called isoflurane began to gently flow. This was to relax him. I thought under the circumstances, this was a very kind thing to do. We both knew a lethal dose of phenobarbital would soon follow.

We said our goodbyes and kissed him on the forehead. My heart was racing even though I knew this was the right thing, the humane thing. As the needle was inserted into a vein in his leg, his breathing slowed for about 20 seconds, then it stopped. He was gone.

I remember his mouth being slightly open and a small bit of his tongue was visible as he breathed his last. In a strange way it was almost cute.

My wife and I looked at each other and our eyes were filled with tears. We'd not expected it to affect us like this. Our hearts were breaking.

I tell you this story about my very first view of death as it occurred to let you know how very much, we loved our cat.

Death is never easy, whether it's a person or an animal. It all hurts. Yes, when a person dies it is much harder because they are us and we are them. Anyone who's ever buried a pet or been through the ordeal I've just described would tell you it's difficult, very difficult. Maybe we're more them and they're more us than we know. It hurts to let them go.

We brought Wicket home and I buried him in the corner of our back yard among several other pets we'd lost over the years. Buried there are mostly cats, but a few bunnies, squirrels and even a sugar glider or two rest in peace 'neath the sod of Seaton Memorial Backyard Pet Cemetery.

We've loved every one of them like family. Because they are.

Sparks of Life

Love takes many forms. You can see it in the eyes of two young people when they look at each other. It's there in the gentle hug from a grandparent who lets us know it's going to be okay. It's certainly in the hearts of the precious animals who live with us.

———

This book is mostly about people and how to learn to live again after they've passed on. Who among us cannot say they truly love their pets? Yes, it's a different kind of love, but it is love.

———

If you've lost someone dear to you, whether a person or a pet, you're experiencing grief and the immeasurable pain of genuine loss. Although humans are harder to lose, be sure to empathize with a friend who's lost an animal. After all, pets are family too.

———

Some perfect tomorrow is impossible to imagine without animals in our lives. These little ones enrich us. They bless us. Love us. The good memories of pets can be just as helpful as other memories. Let the wonder of interacting with these treasured creatures bring you peace. Pet a cat. Watch a goldfish swim. Talk with a parakeet. Rub a puppy's belly.

CHAPTER 11

Road Trip from Heaven

NOT ALL FUNERAL STORIES ARE SAD.

He was lonely for almost 20 years. You could see it in his face, hear it in his voice, and feel it in his hugs. He missed her terribly and he was tired. You don't lose someone you've lived with for 55 years and have it be "business as usual" for the rest of your life. I've never known anyone who has, and I doubt I ever will. I think he was ready to go.

The van was filling up fast. Some luggage placed here, a backpack there, a bag of chips, a few Sony Walkmans tossed under the back seat. It didn't look like there would be any room left for people when all the stuff was loaded.

Anytime you take a trip from Florida to Pennsylvania and your vehicle of choice isn't an airplane, you're looking at a good 20 hours of driving time ahead of you. Over the years, most of the trips were pleasant: a family reunion, a vacation, or just to visit friends and family.

This one was for a funeral. Grandpap died yesterday. After a long and fruitful life, surrounded by his family, he breathed his last—and went Home. He missed Grandma for almost 20 years now. He didn't have to miss her anymore.

It's never easy to lose someone you love, no matter the circumstances. Just because Grandpap was in his 90's didn't mean it didn't hurt us when he died. It did.

Even though funerals are usually sad affairs, once in a while the other stuff related to the funeral isn't. If you've never been in a closed vehicle for 20 hours with 8 other people you need to put it on your Bucket List. There's a special dynamic which happens when several humans are squeezed into a tight space and forced to live in close quarters.

The dynamic takes on a whole different meaning when one of those people sharing the very small space is, well, is having a little problem. On most road trips this long, you'd have to stop for gas at least two or three times depending on your vehicle and how fuel-efficient it is. On this particular journey, they didn't have to stop one single time.

There was enough gas in the van to last them all the way to Pennsylvania. As a matter of fact, there was enough gas inside this van to last these brave travelers the rest of their lives.

It all started with a simple fast food burrito at the first rest-snack-potty break somewhere in South Carolina.

The worst thing of all was, every time "it" started again, no one knew "it" started until it was too late. It would've been nice to get a warning or something. Nope. Just the subtle sensation of your nose telling you it was time to crack open a window.

I guess it was the laughter which was the star of the show. You see, I wasn't on that road trip (yes, there is a God), so this is an "as-told-by" account of the trip to Grandpap's funeral.

The beautiful part of it all is how my wife, her mother, and her sister tell this story through the eyes—and other senses—of those who were in that van. They can't get through the first few lines before they all start laughing so hard, they start to cry.

If you've experienced anything like this, it may not be as funny while it's happening. The priceless gift it becomes for the rest of your life when retelling it almost makes it worth the ride.

It's sad when someone dies, and Grandpap is missed every day. But I wonder if he knows what a priceless gift he left us all. The laughter about a trip to Pennsylvania will never be forgotten by those who experienced it.

And the price of gas will never be the same again.

Sparks of Life

I'm not entirely sure that any kind of "spark" would be a good idea following this particular story.

———

Death is hard, and it hurts like crazy. Life is good and there's always a silver lining if you try hard enough to find it.

———

Laughter is more than just good medicine. It may be the one thing which allows you to keep your sanity when you feel like the world is weighing you down.

———

Some perfect tomorrow is filled with balance. When you're grieving, finding humor in everyday life can give you a lift. You needn't look for the funny. It will find you at just the right time.

CHAPTER 12

Making Memories

Act One:
Valentine's Day

He was lying prostrate. Face-down upon her grave. Weeping. I could hear him on the other side of the cemetery.

In the ancient Hebrew language, there is a word for this. It's called 'al panay (pronounced, "all-pah-'nay").

Derived from the religious concept of "no other god before me," it can also mean face to face, toe to toe, eye to eye, hip to hip, shoulder to shoulder, chin to chin, and breath to breath. As in "let nothing come between us."

Like many eastern languages, the word carries multiple meanings, but one meaning is what this man was doing. His wife died. This was the closest he would ever get to her body again.

Lying flat on the ground. On her grave. Head-to-head. Hip-to-hip. Toe-to-toe. 'al panay.

I'd seen him at the cemetery many times since her death. She was young, he was young. This was one of those hard deaths. I knew it was going to hurt badly. Hurt him it did.

This was a special day for them. It's special for many people who love each other and commit the rest of their lives to each other. This day evolved over 500 years ago from a religious celebration. It's now one in which lovers celebrate their love for each other.

It was Valentine's Day. He was spending this day with his lover, his wife. The one he planned to spend it with the rest of his life.

Love of his life. Mother of his children. Irrevocably separated from him under six feet of earth.

Act Two:
A Cemetery Bench

Every day since he died, she'd come to the cemetery. Every day she sat on the bench near his grave. Every day she talked to him as if he were still alive. Every day.

Today she came with a friend. You can tell a true friend. They're the ones who come to cemeteries with you. You can't put a price tag on this kind of friendship.

Her friend was sitting on the bench. Patting her back. Holding her hair back and stroking her forehead. Today, the bench wouldn't get her close enough.

Today she was kneeling on the ground. In a fetal position. I don't know what the significance of this day was as compared to the others. To her there was something special about it. She needed her friend. She needed some time. She needed some comfort. She needed him.

His grave is close to my mother's. I visited Mom every week after having breakfast with a friend. I'd seen her there. You try not to notice but there's something about grief. Something about someone crying which attracts us. We're drawn involuntarily to crying and mourning. There's something very human about it.

Today as I tried not to notice, I heard her very clearly. "What do you want me to do? What do you want me to do?" She wasn't talking to her friend on the bench.

Over and over she repeated those words. Crying, weeping, rocking back and forth on her hands and knees. All the while, her friend remained silent. Patting her back. Holding her hair. Stroking her head. Being a friend.

Act Three:
Grass-Stained Knees

Mr. Fortenberry was one of the sweetest, gentlest men I ever met. Simple country ways and philosophy on life. They could run circles around the flashiest of modern city-folk thinkers with their complex theories about life and why we're here.

I loved Mr. Fortenberry. He always made time to stop what he was doing and spend a few minutes talking with me. When I stopped by his house every other week or so, he would act as if he hadn't seen me in decades. He'd put down his woodworking tools, give me a big hug and have a Diet Pepsi in my hand lickety-split. We'd spend the next hour rocking on the front porch. Another lost art from a time gone by.

By his cheery demeanor, you wouldn't think this man lost the love of his life, his wife of over 50 years. Not until he started talking about her. If ever there was a woman who was all but worshiped by a man, it was Lilly Fortenberry.

He could be talking about woodworking or his little church family which he loved. Then, in an instant when she crossed his mind he'd drift away and become another person. Eyes misty and distant. It reminded me of the movies when the protagonist gets lost in thought and the scene momentarily fades to another time and place.

Many years ago, early in my funeral career, Mr. Fortenberry was the first person I'd ever seen who would visit a grave and kneel next to the headstone. I never approached him when he was doing this, but I was close enough a few times to hear him speak in his gentle, songlike country tone:

"Now, Sweetie, I wantcha t' know that I'm-a-doing alright. It's hard withoutcha, but I wantcha t' know that I'm okay. I'm-a-gonna make it. It's hard and I miss ya like crazy. I miss ya terrible. I don't wantcha worryin' none about me. I know yer up there in Heaven and God's angels are-a-takin' care o' ya. I love ya Sweetie and I'll see ya soon."

There were deep indentations in the ground right in front of her grave marker where his knees had rested so many times since she died.

The love one person can have for another. On grass-stained knees. On a cemetery bench. On Valentine's Day.

One common thread in these three accounts is they all happened in a cemetery. Cemeteries have a bad rap. Millenia of stories, from ancient generational tales of the dead, to modern-day fantastic Hollywood creations, have mystified and vilified these solemn plots of real estate. Real estate unlike any on earth.

Cemeteries truly are amazing places. They contain amazing stories. They remind us life on Earth is fragile. Extremely fragile, and brief.

They carry with them a greater power than simply a geographical location for interment of human remains. If we let them, cemeteries can help us see life from a new perspective. At least while we find ourselves within their boundaries. The challenge is taking the perspective with us when we glance at the cemetery in our rearview mirrors. Literally and figuratively.

Cemeteries exist because people have loved other people. Even after they died. Especially after they died.

Curtain Call

Although these three acts are about lovers and couples, the truths cemeteries teach us apply to any loss, relationship, circumstance, cause, or any reason your loved one died.

I don't think we can truly know how important it is to embrace the ones we love while we still have them here.

Jim Croce said it well when he wrote about photographs and memories.

After someone we love is gone, memories are all we have left. Let's keep making good ones.

Sparks of Life

For thousands of years of recorded human history, the age-old musings about death remain. What happens when I die? Is this all there is? Does my spirit/soul/essence live on after my physical body dies? Can my ancestors hear my words? Will I hear my descendants'? Impossible to answer. Impossible to not ask.

———

Deep thoughts like these make our lives richer. They are fodder, driving humans forward in search of something more. Something better. They fuel us. Purpose us.

———

See all those names on cemetery headstones and monuments? Every person buried in the graves would urge us to spend our energies thinking these deep thoughts. Advise us to let the petty-minded ones fall to the curb.

———

Some perfect tomorrow is born in love. Love for another human. Love for life. For the beautiful world we've been given. We mix this love with hope and with faith. The result is a powerful push which keeps us going when we think we've gone as far as we can. This push makes us go. We go slowly. Differently. Still, we go.

CHAPTER 13

Words Won't Do

NOBODY KNOWS WHAT TO SAY TO A SURVIVOR when someone they love dies. We try the best we can, but there are no words to accomplish this daunting task. "I'm sorry for your loss." It's likely at the top of the, "I Really Have No Idea What To Say To You" list. While this can gauge what someone's feeling inside (they truly are sorry and they know you've suffered loss), it often sounds canned and insincere.

We don't know what to say, so we do the best we can. We say things like:

"She's in a better place."

"At least he's not suffering anymore."

"Let me know if I can help in any way."

It was early winter when I first met Mrs. Stalling. She was a kind lady from the Midwest in her early 70s. She and Mr. Stalling not only met in high school but dated since the 9th grade. They married during their sophomore year in college. I remember thinking how exceptional this kind of commitment to a relationship was in today's world. They were a couple for the last 50 years. Married for the last 44.

Mr. Stalling was in the air conditioning and heating business. He'd worked hard his whole life to support his family. He was a good husband and father. His mind was a steel trap. He remembered almost every one of his clients' names for the last 40 years. Even more striking, he knew the make and model of the air conditioner unit they had in their homes. Truly amazing.

Like many married couples, when he got home from work each afternoon, he and his wife would spend the first part of their evening asking about the other's day. One day Mrs. Stalling noticed he was struggling with recalling the name of an old client. She shrugged it off because she knew he was tired. It happened three more times the same week.

After a few months of these uncharacteristic lapses she finally convinced him to go to the doctor. Later the blood tests and brain imaging revealed dementia with a suspicion of Alzheimer's. Anyone who's been touched by these terrible diseases would say it's one of the hardest things they've ever dealt with.

Not quite four years from the day his wife noticed he couldn't remember the client's name, George Stalling died. Another life snuffed out by this underhanded mysterious brain disorder. A disease which virtually robs family members of a loved one while they are still alive. An insurmountable foe.

His funeral service was simple.

"That's the way he would've wanted it," Mrs. Stalling told me. "He was a simple man who lived a simple life. Grand ceremonies were not George's style." She glanced at his plain pine casket. Her brow furled as she pursed her lips. A memory played out behind her eyes. Warm smile melted the wrinkles in her brow. "He would love seeing everyone here tonight to honor him. My husband cherished people. I think tonight is perfect."

Her words were sure and proud with a hint of nostalgia. She seemed to remember a time in their lives known only to the two of them.

It was the night before the funeral at Mr. Stalling's visitation when I first began to acutely notice things people say to a survivor. In the funeral home chapel, I made a habit of staying close enough to the next of kin to ensure their needs were met. Yet far enough away to respect their privacy.

I'd also been on the giving end of condolences. I knew the well-wishers were trying their best to come up with words to describe how they felt and give some comfort to the family.

A receiving line was beginning to form as people filed into the foyer. It was about 6:15 and the sun had almost set.

"God bless you, Evelyn," one lady said. She faintly hugged her and quickly moved on. They were obviously close enough for first names but not that close. I assumed she was from Mrs. Stalling's church or maybe a neighbor from a few doors down.

After Church-Neighbor, an older couple came up together. The lady was visibly moved and had an old-fashioned lace handkerchief at the ready. Her husband stood stalwart immediately behind her, hands clasped in front.

"George was a good man," the husband said. He shook Mrs. Stalling's hand while his eyes met hers. "I'll miss him a lot." His wife remained silent, dabbing the corners of her eyes with the handkerchief.

The next young man simply shook her hand, smiled and continued down the line.

Then came one of the most beautiful "condolences" I'd ever seen. No empty words, no formal handshakes. The next person simply stretched out her arms and gave Mrs. Stalling one of the sincerest hugs I think I've ever seen. A purposed embrace.

They held each other for the longest time. When they parted, the woman gave the new widow a small kiss on the cheek. Took her hands in her own, and gave her a look that said, "I'm here." All the while she didn't breathe a word. Not one.

There's a certain kind of closeness with some people. Others are "arm's-length" relationships. We wouldn't expect everyone to express their feelings with a bear hug and a kiss on the cheek.

We should all consider how we relate to the people in our lives—the close ones and the not-so-close. There may come a day when we'll get a handshake and some polite words.

Words and handshakes are nice; but a good hug can steady shaky knees, lighten a weary heart, and prop up a feeble spirit.

Sparks of Life

Death hurts. There are no words to make it otherwise.

⸻

When people speak to you after your loss, understand they don't know what to say and are doing the best they can.

⸻

The next time you have the opportunity to share in someone else's grief, try a silent hug.

⸻

Some perfect tomorrow pivots on the power of human touch. We can embrace technology and still embrace each other. We have at our disposal more words than any time in history. More ways to share words. With over seven billion of us on Earth, we also have more disposable hugs than ever before. The human touch.

CHAPTER 14

Call It Love

WHEN I OPENED THE DOOR TO THE CHURCH, the first thing that caught my eye was the caskets.

Not casket, mind you, but caskets. Two of them. They were the same. Matching colors, matching styles, matching everything, almost. They were perfectly aligned with each other and centered at the front of the room.

In this particular church, there was a beautiful large wooden cross. It hung on the wall behind a small unassuming pulpit. On a normal day, the cross was the first thing anyone would notice when entering the auditorium. The centerpiece.

The cross was background today. Eclipsed by the caskets.

Working in a funeral home, it was not unusual to see two caskets in the same room. It was actually quite common. Those were in the funeral home's casket selection room where families make this difficult choice.

These were very different from the ones found in the selection room, where the caskets were always empty. These caskets were not empty. In these lay two very young people who happened to live in the same small town. They lived on the same street. In the same house, with the same parents, the same siblings and even the same bedroom.

Today, they would share the same funeral. She was 16. Her sister was 14. Even adding their ages together still would have been an unfathomable age to die.

She was driving and her little sister was the passenger. The car crashed on a mountainside one foggy winter morning. Both died instantly. This happy family of eight was, in one terrible moment, transformed into a stunned family of six. Now, two lay in matching caskets with matching colors and matching styles.

I could write words all day long. You and I could read those words over and over again for the rest of our lives. Neither of us would be any closer to making sense out of a story like this. There are not any words invented yet. There never will be.

I wonder what we learn from tragedies like this. If it's learnable at all.

As I entered the building, there was no one else in the room. It was beyond silent. Today, instead of vocationally, I was here as a participant in the service.

The girls' grandfather was a dear friend of mine. He happened to be the pastor of the church. I was one of his lead musicians. The family asked me to perform the piano and vocal music for the funeral.

One of the girls' cousins hurriedly composed a song especially for them and needed my accompaniment. It was a simple, enduring melody with a childlike lyric.

Hours before the funeral was to begin, it was just me and the big empty room and the quiet bodies of two beautiful teenage girls in two matching caskets. It took a long time to take the second step after I'd opened the door and entered the room. I would venture to say most everyone else who walked in experienced the same sensation. I'm not sure if there would be any other way to enter. Burst in? Stroll in? Wander in? No, entering and standing reverently for a moment. It was the only way to enter a room like this.

Perhaps I should go into great detail about the funeral service, but actually I remember very little of it: the caskets, the song, the shock, and the surrealism of the whole event. What I really want to tell you about is their parents.

It is rare when a family member gets up and speaks at a funeral. It's extremely rare when a parent speaks. It's virtually unheard of when both parents do. They did.

These two broken human beings purposely stood in front of several hundred of their closest friends, several dozen of their extended family, and all six of their children. Four sat in the front row, two in caskets. I later learned the mother was expecting her seventh child. She was burying two of her children while life grew inside her.

The father got up and walked to the pulpit. Removing his notes from his jacket pocket, he scanned the audience. A deep breath or two.

"Our girls lived their lives to the fullest," he said. Swallowing hard he looked down at the caskets. "They loved their family." He looked out at the audience. All eyes were upon him. "They loved all of you, too." His voice broke. Tears welled.

His wife put her hand on his shoulder and continued for him. "You could rarely find either of them without a smile on their faces." She found his eyes. He took her hand.

For the next few minutes they somehow read through their notes. Together. One helping the other when words got difficult. They spoke of the one thing which they credited for getting all of them through this terrible time, faith.

Now, it's quite normal at times like these for people to speak of their faith. Death seems to sharpen our focus on life and causes us to ponder it deeper. We really don't think much about living until someone dying makes it unavoidable.

What their mother said next, though, was astonishing.

"We will soon take two of our precious children to the cemetery." She paused and looked at the caskets. She cocked her head. A long breath. She looked down at the front row. Her face beamed. "We are so blessed to take four of them back home."

Tears flooded the audience as she continued. "Loving, nurturing and caring for our remaining four children is our mission now. We'll do it with the same passion and dedication we had when there were six."

In the midst of this family's darkest moment, this loving mother showed all of us in the room a light rarely seen in a public place.

Looking back on the day, I think if only one of her children had survived, she'd have said the same thing. Two young lives were heartbreakingly snuffed out. The two older lives who actually gave life to them, stood brave and stalwart.

It was one of the most beautiful things I ever witnessed in my entire life. I hope I never have to witness it again for as long as I live.

When life dishes out unthinkable, unimaginable events—the sort of stuff which sneaks up on us when we're looking the other way—there is something deep within us which magically wells up and takes us over. Some call it a survival instinct. Some call it a coping mechanism. Others call it higher brain function.

Whatever it is, I saw it glowing in and whirling around and flowing through those parents that day. It was like they were being held up by an invisible force. I'd never seen anything quite like it before and haven't since.

I think I'll just call it love.

Sparks of Life

After a loss—even if you're the very last one left in your family—there are others who still need you. You can find purpose again.

There's a reason you're still here. Don't try to figure out what it is yet. Just knowing this truth is enough for now. The answer to why will come in time, maybe.

Life will never be the same again. It will still be life.

Some perfect tomorrow holds closely to hope. Hope in battered hearts. Hearts of parents who've lost children. Empathy for these produces routine miracles.

CHAPTER 15

But for the Grace

"WE'VE BEEN SAYING GOODBYE for almost 10 years now." She pressed her lips together. Her face sagged. She was exhausted. It showed.

"Were you with him when he died?" I said.

"No. I'd left the room only a moment before. The nurse called me back in—and he was gone."

I'd heard this kind of account of a person's last breath so many times. I wondered if they somehow knew. I knew it must've been hard to say goodbye.

A few weeks earlier this lady came into my office with her adult daughter to make prearrangements for her husband who was in the final stages of Alzheimer's disease. They were married 72 years. Folks have trouble staying together 72 months these days.

She was sprite, sharp, and matter of fact. A tiny bit of a woman—with all her wits and a beautiful head of thick white hair. It gave her the look of an old sage and I thought she must have much to teach. Her browned skin and sinewy limbs showed the outdoor lifestyle she'd enjoyed for almost nine decades. Warren Gamaliel Harding was President of the United States when she was born. So many presidents ago.

She wore faded blue jeans and sneakers. He was 92, she was 89. You don't see a lot of 89-year-olds in faded blue jeans and sneakers. When I first met her, she looked tired. Not from 89 years of life, but from the last 10 years of them preparing for death. His death.

Something in her demeanor said, "I'm ready for him to go." In our contemporary fight-for-every-last-breath-of-life mindset, this may appear as sounding the bugle of retreat. Not for her. She was ready. He was ready. They were all ready.

Even her daughter, who sat quietly through most of our appointment interjected only when her mom needed a reminder of a detail for the vital statistics form. She seemed prepared for her dad's death. They both were. I doubt there are many families of advanced Alzheimer's victims who are not. About two weeks after I helped with the prearrangements, he died.

When I opened the funeral home door, she was just as matter of fact as she'd been before. I gave her a hug which she returned only slightly. After leading them into the same room where they'd been only days ago, we stood for a few minutes and talked. It was there she spoke of "saying goodbye" for almost a decade.

In my profession I've heard many people say many things. They say a lot of the same words, but always in a slightly different way. We are, after all, unique beings, we humans. Some of the sayings, phrases and comments can be predictable. Today, this little woman threw one at me I had not heard before. It stirred some interesting thoughts.

Those of you who are on the other side of death care, hospice, have heard her comment many times. Maybe you've even coached people in how to "say goodbye" to someone while they're still "living."

When she said it to me, my first thoughts were of my own spouse. It's an old and overused maxim to "put yourself in someone else's shoes," but it's old and overused for a reason. It's true. Sometimes it even works. It did on me.

How would I react to this news? What if it was my wife who was diagnosed with this dreaded life-stealer?

She sat still. Collected her thoughts. I asked how she was doing.

"I catch myself reflecting more than usual," she said. "When I was a child, my dear mother used to always say the same thing any time we would come upon a car accident on the road. Any time we saw someone in a wheelchair or an otherwise challenged person."

"'There, but for the grace of God goes you.' Mom would say." Her face lightened as the good memory helped her forget the moment. "She was trying to teach us to be grateful for the wonderful gift of life we were given. To be automatically empathetic. To never again look at someone else's troubles as if 'it could never happen to me.'" She looked straight at me. Her eyes were tired, but strong. Tears flowing.

"I think today I finally learned what my mother was trying to teach us all those years ago." She breathed an extra deep breath. Her whole body relaxed. She dabbed the sides of her eyes with a tissue.

It's impossible to wrestle with these weighty things of life on Earth and not see the deeply spiritual part of just being alive and living life. Today, I felt the pain of another human being. One who said goodbye for the last 10 years to the one she cherished for over 70. It left me with only one solution.

I called my wife and told her I loved her.

Sparks of Life

There's something freeing about accepting things in life over which we have no control. It can even be comforting in some ways. It's where peace lives.

⸻

Your life will never be the same again after the loss of someone you love. It can't be. Some folks may try to tell you otherwise. Smile like you know something they don't. You do.

⸻

You may be a friend to someone who's recently gone through a loss like the one described in this story. One of the best things you can do is let them feel comfortable talking about their loved one. About how different life is without them.

⸻

Some perfect tomorrow can often be difficult to see using the lens of our present life circumstances. The imperfect today actually creates the hope within us. We hope for something better. Something more. Hope will get you through.

CHAPTER 16

Dixie Cups and Details

"WE'VE PLACED MY HUSBAND UNDER HOSPICE CARE, and they've advised us to start making funeral arrangements." Her voice on the phone was hushed, yet strangely confident. "Do you think you could come to the house, so we don't have to come to your funeral home until…well, I mean, until we…."

"Yes ma'am. I'd be glad to. When would you like me to be there?"

"The sooner the better. He's having a pretty good day today."

"No problem. I can be there in an hour. Is that okay?"

"Yes, that would be fine. Thank you so much."

Few things make the wheels of our busy lives (which today, spin at around a million miles-an-hour) grind to a halt like walking into the home of a person who's dying of a terminal illness.

The living room was expertly appointed. It wasn't an overly expensive home as homes go these days, but statelier and more elegant than most. Plush leather sofa, custom window dressings, one of those oversized oil paintings of a departed patriarch hanging above the fireplace. The smart décor reflected the care and loving touches of the lady of the house.

Given her tasteful decorating talents I doubt she would have chosen the grey hospital bed, oxygen machine, and the small table which held the Dixie cup. The Dixie cup which was one third full of saliva.

It was cancer. It was bad. He'd already been through Stages 1, 2 and 3. This was the daunting final number they both knew was bound to come but hoped somehow wouldn't.

I've always thought it remarkable when a person who is dying can teach us so much about what's really important while we're living. This man—though weakened from malnutrition and racked with the pain cancer pounds into the tissues—was one of the most gracious, kind, and loving people I'd ever met.

He waved me over to his bedside and welcomed me with what was once a firm handshake. At first, all I could think of was don't bump the Dixie cup. He smiled a genuine "nice to meet you" smile and motioned for me to sit on the side of the bed and make myself comfortable. I came to make prearrangements for his funeral—and he wanted me to be comfortable.

After exchanging pleasantries, we talked a bit about his life: what he did for a living, his family, where he was born. It doesn't take long when you meet a person like this to see the fruit of a life well-lived. I don't mean well-lived in the financial way. I'm sure he would have traded that overrated commodity for one normal, healthy day now.

No, this life was well-lived in the ways which really mattered. You could see it in his eyes. Especially when he darted them toward his wife. You could sense it when he spoke of his children. You could hear it when his voice broke—not from the cancer affecting his vocal folds, but from the memories he paused to hold before holding them would no longer be possible. He would be the first to tell you it's those things which are the real wealth.

I sat on the edge of his bed the whole time. Where he wanted me to sit. I guided them through the many details: vital statistics, casket choices, cemetery options, even what he wanted on his headstone. I left them with a funeral planning guide so they could later fill in other personal details.

Six weeks later, his wife walked in the front door of the funeral home holding his freshly dry-cleaned suit in one hand. The funeral planning guide in the other. He died about seven o'clock the evening before.

Helping finalize funeral arrangements for someone you've never met, and doing the same for someone on whose bedside you were sitting just a few weeks ago is a much different feeling. Death is always harder the closer you are to someone. I'm glad I was a little closer to this kind man.

It's been many years now since his death. He's interred in the same cemetery as is my mother. When I visit her, I drive by his grave and always glance over at the headstone I designed for him that day. In a flash I'm feeling the weakened handshake. Sitting on the edge of his bed and trying very hard not to spill the Dixie cup.

Sparks of Life

The experts call it "anticipatory grief." It's knowing what you're facing and missing someone while they're right there in front of you. Another word for it is "love."

There are well-meaning people in your life who will try to fill the void. You know they can't. If they're honest, they probably know it too. Let them try anyway and just be as gracious as you can. They're doing the best they can just like you are.

If you were the long-term caregiver for a loved one who passed away, you may find yourself not knowing what to do with your "extra" time. Don't try to solve the puzzle too quickly. As impossible as it seems right now, it will solve itself.

Some perfect tomorrow grows as a towering oak when caregivers do what they do. Givers of help. Of hope. Of their very selves. Bless the caregivers. They lasso some perfect tomorrow and reel it in. For today.

CHAPTER 17

The Face of an Angel

I ALMOST TRIPPED OVER IT as I walked the cemetery. Huddled amongst a clump of weeds snubbed by the lawn mower was a barely legible tin nameplate sticking out of the ground.

It measured about ten inches wide by four inches high and was affixed to a metal stake driven into the ground. The nameplate was kept company by a broken ceramic angel surrounded by discarded ornaments from a distant Christmas. These signs are placed by funeral homes immediately after a burial to temporarily mark the grave until a proper headstone is installed.

I bent over to brush off the dirt so I could see the name and cut my finger on its sharp metal edge. A reflexive finger into mouth produced an interesting childhood memory. The taste of dirt mixed with blood.

The letters and numbers were barely legible. Faded by years of bright Florida sunshine.

Judith L. Riggins

3-12-38 – 11-5-92

Chapman Brothers Funeral Home

The day I nearly stumbled upon the little sign was Wednesday, March 5, 2012. Miss Riggins had died almost 20 years earlier. She wasn't alone. There were hundreds, maybe thousands of people buried all around her. This was a cemetery after all.

In a graveyard, you can find some pretty amazing headstones and monuments which families erect to memorialize their departed loved ones. From the very simple to the extremely ornate. These granite and marble monoliths stand for centuries and somehow connect the dead with the living.

I'm sure, at least in my eternal optimism, Miss Riggins' family loved her as much as the rest of these surrounding families loved their own Miss Rigginses.

On a few graves to the right stood a huge jet-black granite headstone. It loomed like a sentry on duty, guarding the residents at its feet. On its front was a meticulously detailed color scene, hand-etched by a very talented artist. Green foliage, a little white church and a peaceful pond surrounded the images of two people walking hand-in-hand into a stunning sunset. The creator of this headstone made it more a work of art than a grave marker.

In the upper middle of the granite was a full-color oval porcelain cameo of a man and a woman. Even though she died in the 1990s, from the light blue leisure suit worn by the man, her ruffled dress, and some atrocious hairdos for both, this photo was surely straight out of the 1970s.

On either side of the headstone, matching granite flower vases contained freshly cut flowers. There were even a few drops of dew still on some of the rose pedals. At closer glance,

I realized they were silk flowers with crafty spots of acrylic to mimic dewdrops. The back of the stone listed the names of their children and grandchildren. All carved in granite, all literally etched in stone recording this family's heritage.

I glanced back over at Miss Riggins' grave. The broken angel hadn't even noticed I wasn't paying much attention to her resident's burial plot. She continued to hold what was left of a small harp and looked heavenward. Even though only about half her face remained. The other half lay broken, upside down on the ground at the feet of a little faded teddy bear wearing an even more faded Santa hat.

I took a moment and considered both burial sites. Always the underdog's greatest advocate, my heart felt for Miss Riggins and her family. I pondered the circumstances which left her grave with nothing more than this tin nameplate for so many years.

Did the family have no money? Could they not agree on what to write for her epitaph? Had they moved away after she died and forgotten about her? It was possible she simply had no family left. Maybe she was the last one.

I'm no socialist, but I have been accused of a bit of socialistic ideology in my day. Something inside me screams when class inequality triumphs. I know, I know, the world isn't fair. The poor live alongside the rich.

Large black granite stones will always share cemeteries with small tin markers in the same way 15,000 square foot mansions with a Bentley in the driveway are often only a five-minute drive from a rusty 82' Chevette parked next to a dilapidated single-wide.

Philosophy, economics and fair play aside, I think everyone deserves more than a little tin sign to mark the place where their mortal remains will forever lay. Even if those remains will eventually dissolve back into the earth from whence they came. As these grand thoughts were swirling inside my head, I swirled the outside of it and looked at the other graves.

Miss Riggins wasn't the only one with a tin marker. There were several more scattered here and there. I strolled over to look at a few.

Even before reading the dates, it was clear these were fresh burials. A few still had the dirt mounded, meaning the grave had yet to settle. January 2012. November 2011. December 2011. These recent interments were likely waiting for the granite company to install the headstones. Or maybe not.

Maybe Miss Riggins started out this way 20 years ago.

This story does have a happy ending though. I copied down her name and dates and the name of the funeral home. After a few days of research, I found Mr. Riggins. We talked a while on the phone. I told him I'd like to help him get a monument for his wife.

He turned out to be one of the sweetest people. He was a simple, big-hearted person who lived way below what is commonly called the poverty level. Way below. He thought a headstone was something he could never afford.

Mrs. Riggins now has a permanent headstone marking her grave. I designed a simple affordable monument for his wife. He was able to make small monthly payments and stay within his humble fixed income budget.

No, it's not a jet-black monolith with hand-etched scenery. There is no porcelain cameo portrait of his youthful bride and no fancy flower vases. But there was one thing which pleased him greatly. He told me his wife loved anything to do with angels, hence the tattered one I found at her grave.

The tin sign and the Santa bear finally found their way to the county landfill. Mrs. Riggins' name and dates are forever etched into a beautiful Georgia Grey granite monument. Right above her first name is a nice little angel carved right into the stone.

I don't think this one's face will ever fall off.

Sparks of Life

Being remembered is a basic human need. Deep inside, we all fear being forgotten. Cemeteries are one way to perpetuate these memories. Visit them when you can.

⚌

We all know the person who has died is not there in the grave. The animating force which made them who they were left when they breathed their last. Still, there's a delicate sense of life's brevity when we ponder it in the confines of a graveyard.

⚌

Cemeteries don't have to be sad places. As with anything in our lives, they can be used for good. Take your children or grandchildren there. Even if you visit a cemetery where none of your family's buried, it's a fitting chalkboard filled with teachable moments and not just for the kids.

⚌

Some perfect tomorrow remembers. If it achieves nothing else, it remembers. It may well be the entire sum of our memories. Private and shared. How precious a gift. Memory. Cherish its wonder.

CHAPTER 18

Mrs. Green's Coffee

THE FUNERAL HOME DOOR FINALLY OPENED. She stood motionless, holding her husband's dated pinstriped suit. Never worn. It looked more at home in its "A-1 Dry Cleaners" bag than it ever would on him.

In her other hand she held a weathered manila folder with paperclip-shaped rust stains along its top edge. Some dog-eared papers peeked out the corners. Behind her a few adult children stood. Their heads lowered, eyes blank, hearts heavy. As if on cue, the sun went behind the clouds. A stormy breeze ruffled their mom's skirt which was as motionless as she was.

He'd died sometime during the night. The husband, father, and grandfather who held this family so tightly together all these years became the next statistic in the county's mortality records.

Walking through the door of a funeral home is never an easy thing to do. We seem to evade this particular door until the very last and final moment. Even then, only when we can shirk it no longer. It's akin to visiting a cemetery or a hospital. No one really does it unless they're forced by circumstance.

Over the next hour or so, this precious family of three, which, less than 12 hours ago was a completed family of four, would come face-to-face with reality. Harsh reality. They would be forced and forged by this uncaring and cold-hearted foe called circumstance.

Circumstance would compel them to make extremely difficult and heart-wrenching decisions on one of the hardest days of their lives. Decisions made when their hearts were wounded beyond any hope of ever healing. At least, that's what it felt like at the time.

Funny character, this fellow known as Circumstance. He doesn't seem to care one iota who falls desperately into his path. He's purely and unashamedly unemotional, apolitical, and irreligious. He does not discriminate.

Mrs. Green handed me the freshly dry-cleaned suit. I took it from her as I gave her a sincere hug which let her know this was a safe place. She lingered in my arms for a moment. I escorted the family into the arrangement room and offered coffee, water or soft drinks.

"Yes, I'd like some coffee," she said. There was a hint of normalcy in her voice.

I thought how something as simple as a cup of coffee had the power to bridge some mystical gap between "he's gone" and "I remember when we used to…."

A sepia image danced from left to right in my mind. My wife and me sitting in our backyard enjoying our morning coffee. It's funny, how when we feel out of control, something familiar and routine helps somehow.

"You know," she said with a distant tone, "Hal and I always said we were going to talk about our final arrangements one day. We had planned on sitting down at the kitchen table and really planning out what we would do if one of us..." She bit her lip and looked away.

She tried to complete the thought. It wouldn't come. It was tough. She glanced back and I told her with my eyes I knew it was hard.

"...if one of us...died." She finished the thought. Her tears welled and momentarily stayed at the critical point before spilling over the lower eyelids. When eyelids had done their valiant best, they succumbed and allowed the tears to go their way. These were tears of finality, of fear, of uncertainty and, of love. It showed.

"I never thought I would have to go through this by myself. We always joked we would just go to sleep one night and never wake up. I guess that's what everyone would like."

I rendered a half-smile to let her know I had no response.

Martha Green was facing the very real vision of what the rest of her life would look like without Harold Green sharing it. It was sobering.

I'd seen this played out so many times, but each time it seemed to be brand new. Like it was the very first time I'd ever helped a family who'd lost a loved one. It was not. No, I'd done this a thousand times before. I've always prayed I never get used to what I do. Never get used to the human part of my job. For Martha the hard part was still ahead. As a matter of fact, lots of hard parts were still ahead.

After we completed the vital statistics, I asked the question which always led to how the remaining questions would be answered. There would be many decisions made in the next hour or so, but we started with this huge one.

"Have you chosen burial or cremation?"

"Burial," said Mrs. Green. Her eyebrows curled. She held her chin, resting her index finger between her lips. Burial was a hard word.

More than an hour later, this funeral arrangement which started out so routinely took a sad and heartfelt turn. It was a turn I'd seen so many times before and dreaded every time I saw it coming.

Mr. Green had a life insurance policy. Not much. I think it was around $10,000, just enough to "put him away" as he'd hinted during their 25 years together. They had very little in savings, not the greatest credit, and no source of income, other than Hal's weekly paycheck from the construction company. Now, Harold Green would never deposit one of those checks again.

The funeral director stood up. "If you'll excuse me, I have some paperwork to complete." The director took the insurance policy and walked upstairs to the business office. She would complete forms for Mrs. Green to sign and call the insurance company to validate the policy.

After several minutes the funeral director came back into the arrangement room. Her expression didn't look promising.

The fear on Mrs. Green's face added about 10 years to her age as the funeral director announced the sad news. Hal's life insurance policy lapsed about a year ago for lack of premium payment.

It seems Mr. Green, who took care of all the bills, had to make a choice. Keep them in their home by making the mortgage payment or pay the life insurance premium. In his mind the choice was clear. They needed a place to live and they could always get another policy once things picked up again at work.

Things never picked up again at work. The Greens stayed in their home and the insurance company cancelled their policy. It wasn't worth the paper it was printed on.

It happens every day. Hurting people, forced by circumstance to make impossibly difficult decisions. Then having to figure out how they're going to pay for the final arrangements.

I thought about all the times when families experienced a death and had the forethought to prepay their arrangements years before. How much easier this day would have been on Martha Green.

Sparks of Life

In the death care profession, we see a different view than virtually anyone else in any other profession. Families facing the unthinkable sit across the table from us every single day. It makes sense to plan for your final arrangements. It's not hard. In fact, it's quite simple.

If you're reading this book, there's a good chance you've lost someone in your life. The pain can be anywhere from manageable to unbelievable. Even if you've not lost a loved one or friend, give some thought to making advanced plans for yourself.

One of the most popular responses I hear when asking people if they've taken care of their final arrangements in advance is, "I have life insurance." Good. Keep your policies in force. Life insurance was never intended to pay for your final expenses. It's meant to take care of your family after you're gone.

Some perfect tomorrow can get you through a difficult day. Moment. Heartbeat. In perilous times people have held on to hope against all odds. Hold on.

CHAPTER 19

Coffin Full of Hope

CASKETS SHOULD HAVE WARNING labels like any other manufactured product.

The label on a casket should read:

WARNING: THIS PRODUCT IS NOT INTENDED FOR PERSONS UNDER THE AGE OF 90. ALWAYS KEEP AWAY FROM CHILDREN.

In the world of funeral providers, our service does not discriminate based on race, gender, religion, social status or age. Today, the person occupying this casket was only 20 years old. The one responsible for putting him there had ignored the label.

It was Saturday evening. The rest of the staff all left around 4 o'clock, so I had the whole funeral home to myself. The public viewing would begin at six. The immediate family would arrive an hour prior for their private time.

I'm guessing you've never been by yourself in a funeral home. It's an interesting experience. There's something about being alone in a quiet room with a dead person lying in a casket which is holy. Sacred. You feel like whispering, even though there's no one there to hear even if you screamed.

Because this young man was exactly my son's age, and because, this was the very first time I took care of a family whose 20-year-old son died, this was difficult. Very difficult. You'd think you would get used to this after many years in the business. You don't. I hope I never do.

I won't go into the details of this death except to say, like many deaths, this one was preventable. Absolutely preventable. While they never proved there was any foul play, the parents of this young man still think there was. They live daily with those nebulous "facts" in the police report. The gaping blank space in Block #41 on the death certificate. Block #41 is for the doctor to list the cause of death. No one is sure what happened to him, so the line remains blank.

It was just the two of us in the room. I felt compelled, even somehow drawn to approach his casket. Not merely to stare. He looked like he was sleeping. How many times have you heard someone say this about a person lying dead in a casket? "They looked like they were asleep." It's not always true the deceased appear to be sleeping. Sometimes they look like they're dead. Not this one. He was just sleeping.

I first felt the urge from somewhere deep in my abdomen. Like a low hunger pang. It grew in intensity. When fully matured, it squeezed me, then released its hold. I wept.

I thought about this young man's life, his childhood, dreams and aspirations. I thought about his mom and dad. It hit me. The full force of this young man's death hit me way before I was ready for it. Whatever "it" was didn't care if I was ready or not.

I spent a long time thinking about and personalizing the scene before me. I couldn't stop. I wanted to stop, but I chose not to. I was compelled to fully empathize with his parents before I could walk away from the casket and prepare myself to comfort the family later in the evening.

If I didn't know any better (and I may not have) I was compelled somehow to envision my own 20-year-old child in the casket before I could move on. My child. Not theirs. Mine. It was at this moment the thought came.

I am going to place my hands on this boy's chest and ask God to breathe life back into him. I am going to raise this young man from the dead. There's really no other option. He must live again.

If you think the last paragraph sounds strange, you're correct. Strange or not, it's exactly what I did. Maybe it was faith or just plain foolishness. I was going to boldly ask. If there was a God listening to me, I wanted to be sure he knew I meant business.

The young man's chest was firm and cool to the touch. He was dressed only in a t-shirt and jeans, so there wasn't a lot of cotton in between his skin and my palms. Palms which were now sweating a lot.

I placed both hands squarely on his sternum, and I prayed. I didn't roll my eyes back in my head or say some magic words or even quote something that sounded spiritual. I just argued with God.

"This would be no big deal for you, but it would be a huge deal for this boy's family. An enormous deal."

Then, I simply asked for his life to return to him.

It was barely noticeable at first. I felt the slightest warmth begin to return to his body as blood started to circulate again. The hardness of his chest eased off a little and was replaced with the subtle elasticity of muscle tissue beneath skin. Then as if on cue his chest began to slowly rise.

The diaphragm drew air through his nostrils and began filling the lungs. My eyes then left his sternum and made an unhurried pan to the left. I wanted to be focused and ready when the Windows of the Soul made their grand entrance into the room. I was looking directly into those young eyes when they opened ever so slowly and looked squarely into mine.

That's exactly the way it happened until the instant I removed my hands, turned around and sat down on the front pew of the chapel. I was drained and exhausted.

It happened only in my mind.

As I sat there, his body was just as still as the moment the life left it a few days before.

Is there a moral to this story? A lesson? Yes.

There will come a day for you and for me when our own bodies will become irrevocably still. Even so, there remains something in all of us who want to believe in miracles like this. If you're honest, you may even admit something inside you was happening as you read those words a moment ago.

I think it's the one thing that makes us human more than any other trait. Hope.

Sparks of Life

Hope is not some distant and unattainable longing. It's a very real force somehow wired into our makeup as human beings. It gives us strength to go on.

Losing someone we love dearly can feel like all hope is lost. It's not. The hope you shared when they were alive is still there. Yes, maybe it will be different, but you still have it.

There will probably be days when you don't even feel like getting out of bed. "What's the use?" can sound like such a practical, even comforting question. If your lost loved one could tell you, they'd answer, "The 'use' is you. Go be hope for someone else."

Some perfect tomorrow thrives upon expectations, even daydreams. Imagining a better day is not fantasy. Our feelings of future goodness can help in our present uncertainty. Sustain us in the now. Keep on daydreaming. It's good for you.

CHAPTER 20

Shaken

IF THERE WAS A WEBSITE NAMED www.strange-but-true-funerals.com, this one would be a contender.

The funeral director's walk began in the back of the church. His brisk, stately pace up the center aisle was perfect. His gait, purposed. His impeccable timing—which put him already well in stride at the second syllable of the prayer's amen—would make Britain's famous train system blush.

Followed by his assistant, they arrived at the open casket and began this ritual for the thousandth time. Reverently, the assistant lifted the flower blanket and held it to the side while the director folded in the casket's velvet material. Holding the lid with his right hand, the funeral director tripped the latch and closed the casket. His assistant replaced the flowers. Completing the somber ritual.

This is a solemn time. For many families, one of the most telling in the entire funeral process. This is when they see their loved one's body for the very last time—ever. The final time. It's the end. It's difficult. At this moment, no one would dare drop a pin for fear everyone would hear it. There's not a single eye looking elsewhere.

This funeral service was emotional from the start. Very emotional. At this particular service you could have dropped several truckloads of pins and no one would have noticed.

She missed her mama. Boy, how she missed her mama. Being a grown woman didn't make one single bit of difference. She wailed like a little girl. She shrieked like a Halloween witch. Several times she threw herself on her mother's body lying motionless in the casket. She moaned and cried and squalled and mourned in most every discernible way. Until everyone in the church was on edge.

"This-is-my-mama." She screamed. The volume level of her voice doubled. Raspy from crying. She turned to face the crowd. She scolded them. Her index finger wagging. "I couldn't care less what any of you hypocrites think." Both index fingers now working. She lowered her head and glared at them. Looking over her glasses. "You all sit there staring at me. Judging me. Still hurting me..." Her words disappeared into another weeping session. Moaning. Hurting. Spewing.

In a way, it was kind of cool. Not cool in the hipster way; but cool she felt free enough—even in front of all these people—to express herself with such abandon. She had a lot of stuff stored up inside her. It needed to come out.

At a traditional funeral, several distinct occurrences seem to help survivors gain closure of the death. I call these defining points. This final lowering of the casket lid is one of the most poignant. It speaks, screams, and sometimes whispers volumes of the finality of the person's life. It's a tough scene to resolve.

The family and friends, the funeral home staff, and even the preacher were all a bit relieved when the daughter started to calm down a little as we processed out of the church. We walked to the hearse and began our trip to the cemetery.

Although it does happen, it's rare for the casket to be reopened at the graveside after the procession arrives at the cemetery. Rare indeed. For a reason.

The pall bearers completed their slow walk from the hearse to the gravesite. Timing their steps. Looking straight ahead. Each responsible for one sixth of the casket's burden. Left. Right. Left. Attendees found their graveside seats under the large green tent. The tent's edge featured the funeral home's name printed on one side. Artificial grass served as a temporary carpet for the 20 or 30 metal folding chairs. Green velvet slip covers on each chair. Crisp white letters on the front row covers read, "RESERVED FOR FAMILY."

Everyone was seated. The daughter remained standing. She turned to the funeral director.

"Mr. Alderman, please open my mother's casket again. I want to see her one final time." Her voice was calm and reserved. She blinked a few times and took a deep breath. It was the quietest she'd been all day. The last syllable was barely out before she started crying again.

The funeral director seemed to object with his eyes but obliged her request. With dignity he motioned for his assistant. They reversed the entire process they'd just performed in the church.

He opened the casket. Unfolded the velvet. Locked the casket lid in its open position. Once again revealing its occupant. He stepped away and looked at the daughter. Nodded his head.

She moved in. Embracing the casket. More wailing. More crying. More mourning.

The attendees stood in disbelief. Their faces wrinkled up. A few heads tilted. Muffled words waltzed through the group. "What did she just say?" "Huh?" "Why, I never..." "Doesn't she know that..."

After a few minutes the daughter's emotions were apparently drained from her—and everyone else. The committal portion of the funeral ended. Folks started talking, mingling, and hugging. Even smiling. Soft laughter could be heard. There's an almost plausible group exhale when the cemetery burial element of a funeral is over. It's another defining point.

The daughter chose to be the first one to leave and did so post haste. She opened the passenger door and got in her boyfriend's car. He ushered her away from her mother's final resting place. Tires squealing blue smoke mixed with exhaust into the still morning air.

Everyone at the gravesite jerked their heads in unison to see what was happening. A small child was startled by the sudden sound and started crying. The boyfriend was in such a rush, his car almost struck the funeral director's assistant who was escorting an elderly lady to her vehicle.

The emotions we all thought cleaned her soul and exhausted the rest of us reared their heads for one last episode. Scarcely 20 feet away, she was literally hanging out the car window.

"You never loved her like I love her." Yelling, screaming, howling at the top of her lungs. "You just used her and abandoned her. You left her all by herself." Tossing the F-Bomb, with all its quaint variations. Sometimes every third or fourth word. "I hope I never see you again." The daughter screamed an agonizing scream. "I hope you all choke to death!"

She sounded hoarse. Coughing. Crying. Somehow managing to fit an F-Bomb between each of her final words. She rendered middle finger salutes to everyone in her family. Her voice lingered. Faded into the distance.

A haunting quiet hovered the crowd. Everyone wanted to say something. No one did. They all looked at each other. A few shook their heads. Some scratched theirs. Eyebrows raised. Wide-eyed expressions of disbelief. Indignation.

As the silence broke a few folks spoke in hushed tones. Most returned to their conversations, ignoring the daughter's antics. Some laughter returned and lightened the mood. It seems they were not surprised by her emotional outbreaks.

If we're honest, we can see ourselves in this story. Anger is a perilous bedfellow with sorrow. Each of us deals with these two emotions differently. Our reaction to loss is never predictable. We wouldn't be human if it was. Whatever a person has stored up inside will come out when they are shaken.

Sparks of Life

Grief surfaces feelings in a way no other experience can. Understanding this can help make sense of things when nothing makes much sense.

If you've experienced a loss you've most likely discovered emotions you never knew you had. From excessive sadness to outright rage, these are all normal feelings. Don't let anyone tell you otherwise.

After moments like this pass, even if it happens when you're alone, it's natural to feel embarrassed and even a little ashamed. Use the time to take a step back and appreciate yourself for who you are, warts and all.

Some perfect tomorrow offers us priceless empathy. Even for people like the daughter in this story. We can never know what another has endured. What made them the way they are. The least we can do is love them. The most we can do is love them.

CHAPTER 21

The Last Six Feet

THE HUNTER GREEN CANVAS CEMETERY tent tried its man-made best to blend into nature under those towering ancient oaks. The wise old trees saw the tents come and go. Several times a day for many, many years. Every time there was another burial, these tents were erected over the graves providing temporary shelter for the casket and a few dozen chairs.

It was early in my career as a funeral professional. Maybe my second or third week on the job. I was cruising this massive cemetery in a golf cart to familiarize myself with its many sections: The Hope Garden; The Garden of the Good Shepherd; The Jewish Garden; the private mausoleum areas; the cremation columbaria.

Parked beside this particular tent was the classic black hearse or "the coach" as it's called in the funeral profession. There's something about seeing one of those long black cars that always turns heads no matter where it's spotted. The sight of a hearse commands a strange awe coupled with a sobering mystique, even in a cemetery, where it should look natural. This particular coach was empty.

The burnished steel casket was precisely positioned directly above the grave on the mechanical lowering device. It was decidedly still. Devoid of emotion, this casket seemed to be patiently waiting to escort its occupant on his final trip on Earth. This trip would be barely six vertical feet from start to finish.

As I rounded the corner, I saw two funeral home personnel garbed head to toe in more classic black. They were getting ready for the service before the family and friends of the deceased were to arrive. This is what's commonly referred to as a graveside service. Rather than a church, synagogue or funeral chapel, some families choose to simply meet at the cemetery to honor their departed loved one. An outdoor funeral.

The hearse driver was flagging me over.

What in the world does he want with me? I'm the new guy.

"Good morning young fella," the elder of the two said. He almost sang in a deep southern drawl. He bent forward and offered me a hearty handshake. "Would you be willing to help us for a moment?"

"Of course, I'd be happy to."

I still couldn't imagine what they wanted. Maybe they need me to run back to the office for some flowers they'd forgotten. Yes, that was it. There were none of the usual floral arrangements surrounding the casket. It could be the flowers were on the way and they just wanted to meet the new guy.

"We were wondering if you would be so kind as to sign this man's register book. We two have already signed it and you see, well, no one else is coming to the funeral. This is it."

This is it? Is that what he really said?

"I'm sorry. Did you say no one is coming to this person's funeral?"

The southern gentleman gave me a soothing look. Years of smiling carved lines into the corners of his eyes. Sky blue irises contrasted his dark suit. I guess he'd seen raised eyebrows and gaping mouths like mine before. I scratched my head. Pocketed my freshly shaken right hand.

"Yeah, pretty sad isn't it? This guy obviously had nobody. According to his info sheet, he's only 68. I guess all his family either lives out of town or just doesn't care, or both. Anyway, we thought the least we could do is sign his register book before they lower him down."

Who gets the register book if there's no one to attend his burial?

In the distance I heard the hum of the backhoe used to complete the burial by filling in the grave with earth. I looked around once more. Only the backhoe was coming. There was no one else. It was just us three and the mortal remains of a fourth.

In life, there are those times when you feel like a fish out of water. There are other times when you feel like an actor in a badly scripted movie. This was both. I wanted to cry. I wanted to shout out loud, but I didn't know what to shout.

I thought briefly about looking up the family's phone number and telling them what terrible people they were for not being here. I wanted to look across the way and finally sigh with relief as I saw cars meandering through the cemetery carrying family and friends to this man's final resting place. No one was coming. I stood there with the only other people on earth who had come to witness the burial—all two of them.

Why was there no one here? It could be this man alienated his family. He alienated them to the point none wanted to say their last goodbyes? Or to honor 68 years lived? Or recognize his contribution to the world? Maybe it was his fault. Even so, no one should have to go this last voyage alone. Not this journey.

Something in me clicked that day. No angels sang. I didn't raise a finger to my chin and whisper, aha! I didn't hear the orchestra crescendo. But something happened inside—something which lingers to this day.

I wondered how many people are just like this guy. If it's too late for some of them. If his life could have been different. Especially the end of it. I wondered if there's still time to make sure there are more than three people at my funeral.

Sparks of Life

No one really wants to be lonely. It's okay to be alone, everybody needs time to themselves. But no one should have to spend the end of their lives like this.

If you know someone who has no one, take a few minutes and let them know you're there if they need you.

Do all within your power, for the rest of your life, to ensure there are more than three people who will miss you when you're gone.

Some perfect tomorrow carries with it the solution to loneliness. Empathy. It creates space for understanding others. Especially the lonely.

CHAPTER 22

Mrs. Wilkins' Appointment

HER LEFT ARM WAS CLUTCHED TO HER CHEST. She held a paper-stuffed folder with a faded business name printed in gold letters on the front. Decades faded. It was a cold day, very cold. An unexpected breeze tightened her grip, keeping the papers from becoming unruly kites. In her other hand, the remains of her husband.

His ashes fit nicely into a small plastic container about the size of a shoebox. The container was carefully placed in what resembled a black shopping bag. The kind with twine handles and a business's logo imprinted on one side. This particular logo belonged to the local funeral home.

Her trip from the building to the sidewalk was much slower today than the last time. Her pace was measured. She'd never dreamed of doing this—at least not alone. Today, she was very much alone.

As she exited the funeral home, a man inside watched her every step through the pane glass door.

The tightly clutched papers bustled in the wind. The black shopping bag in her right hand swung in rhythm with her steps. Her car stood empty in the parking lot.

There was no one else in sight, no one waiting for her to return. Only a single person populated this parking lot. Carrying what remained of another person. In a box. A person in a box—inside a bag.

The cremated remains of an adult human being are about the size and weight of a five-pound bag of sugar. It's ironic the physical appliance which carries around our thoughts, hopes, dreams, and our very soul from embryo to adulthood, can be reduced to a bag of anything. Look in a mirror. You fit in a bag.

She'd arrived at my office a short while ago on business. There were papers to sign. Certificates to explain. Identification to verify. Business. Part of the business involved delivering to her the cremated remains of her husband.

"Hello Mrs. Wilkins," I said. "How are you this afternoon?"

"I'm doing all right, I guess. Taking it one day at a time." Her eyes lowered. No need to elaborate. This wasn't the time or the place for chitchat. This was a tough day. As if any of the last several were easy.

"Please have a seat. May I offer you a bottle of water?"

"No, thank you." Mrs. Wilkins went to place her folder on the table before sitting down. It slipped out of her hands and landed with a heavy smack. She trapped the contents with both hands just as they were about to fly away. She looked up at me. Her eyes seemed tired.

We settled into our places at the table. I let her know what to expect. Our staff was always careful to paint a picture of what would transpire in the next few minutes. Let the family member know we valued their loved one. It seemed to lessen the shock. A little.

She took it well. Seeing what was left of her husband's body. In a little plastic box.

In a few minutes our business was complete. I gave her a hug and offered to escort her to her car. She politely declined. I understood. The lonely walk.

The man peering out the pane glass door was me. As I watched her, the emotions I'd been holding in wanted out. You know how it feels when a cry starts, don't you? Your throat tightens and your brow bends upward a little between your now-misty eyes, which are wetter by the moment.

And then it comes. And it hurts a bit. Physically hurts.

You may think, "Hey, this guy works at a funeral home. He must cry all the time." Yes, it's a sad thing to witness death's effect on people. Sure, I cry. Not every time, but I still do. We all do. Anybody in this profession who says otherwise is either a liar or needs to think about a new job.

Today, as Mrs. Wilkins walked away carrying the cremated remains of Mr. Wilkins, I didn't cry because she lost her husband. I don't even think it was empathy. It was because this was all she had left of his body.

The real sadness of this story was not so much Mr. Wilkins' death. It was Mrs. Wilkins' aloneness. Maybe she wanted to come by herself to get his ashes. It's possible.

It would be easier to believe if someone had been with her last week. When she came to the funeral home to make the arrangements. There wasn't.

Or if someone had escorted her on the day of the memorial service. They didn't.

Or if someone held her hand as she walked away from the cemetery. After the final prayer was said. No one did.

There was a good reason none of this happened. She had come alone to make the arrangements. There was no need for an escort because there was no memorial service. A cemetery wasn't needed since there was no burial to have a final prayer after.

She chose what is called a "basic" or "direct" cremation. No memorial service, no viewing, no burial, no flowers, no casket. Nothing.

It reminded me of something I've heard many times in casual conversations. "What, me? Heck, I just want to be cremated. I don't want anyone fussing over me when I die. When I'm dead, I'm dead you know? Send me flowers while I'm living." We are free to choose.

Freedom has its perks. Choosing not to have a funeral or celebration of the end of someone's life is one of them. Choosing to just keep plowing through life as if nothing even happened is another perk. Funny thing. Freedom and its perks. Mrs. Wilkins didn't look very free today.

Loneliness disguises itself in many forms. Maybe freedom is one of them.

We celebrate many important events in life. Does the end of life deserve any less? I'll bet the Wilkins Family stopped their routines many a time to celebrate a birthday, graduation, wedding, promotion, retirement, anniversary, or even a friend's divorce. Why didn't they stop and celebrate this time?

One of the hardest funerals I've ever attended wasn't one.

Sparks of Life

Take time to celebrate the life of someone who's passed on. It's okay. Celebrate.

Consider inviting some friends and family to a purposed event. One intended to remember a precious life lived. It doesn't have to be fancy—just purposed.

Set aside some private time for you to celebrate their memory. Just you. Alone with their memory. Every day of your life.

Some perfect tomorrow will never question you or your motives. It is a good place. A place where your should-haves fade into doesn't-matters. The kind of place where healing happens. Good happens. Life happens.

CHAPTER 23

Chesters and Carters

"**Y**OU SHOULD HAVE BEEN HERE LAST NIGHT for that visitation," the funeral director said. "You couldn't fit another single person in the chapel. It was packed. He must've been a good guy."

Barely a week earlier this same director stopped me at the Monday morning coffeepot. "Tisk, tisk," his lips smacked. He shook his head from side to side. His squinting eyes revealed a tale of woe on the way.

"Boy, it sure was a small funeral yesterday," he said. He stirred his cup and cocked his head. Famous left eyebrow rais-ing halfway to his hairline. "I could count on one hand the folks who came to pay their respects. So sad." His overfilled cup sloshed as he turned to walk down the hall. Coffee creamer spots marked his morning soapbox.

There are some like this funeral director who feel the need to measure most everything. I guess we all do to some extent. As hard as we may try not to, we make judgments about people every day. Some of this is just plain necessary to function normally—such as making sure the driver of that truck makes eye contact with you before you start to cross the street.

Some judgments we make are based on much less dependable data than making a decision about whether or not it's safe to enter the crosswalk.

Some, like my colleague's judgments at the coffee pot, would measure the worth of a life by the number of people who show up at the end of it to say a last goodbye, or as the old saying goes, pay their respects. It's just not so.

Molly Carter was a brand-new widow. She was standing inside the funeral home chapel door greeting everyone with a strained smile as they filed in for the 10 a.m. ceremony. Her tailored black suit perfect. Her small frame raised a few inches by matching heels.

The last 72 hours were a blur. They seemed more like a movie than real life. Three days, 12 hours and 15 minutes ago she and her husband, Bill were on their way home from a nice dinner with her parents when the deer darted out of the woods. Couple the lightning speed of a deer with the 65 miles-per-hour momentum of a large SUV and little could've been done to avoid the accident. Bill Carter tried his best to avoid a collision.

"It all happened so fast." Molly said. She sat across the table from me at the funeral home. "I remember Bill's arm instinctively flying across my chest."

Her arm tensed as she waved her arm out. She braced it against the chair next to her as one would a small child. Imaginary passenger seat. Her head dropped.

"I wonder if that's why I survived, and he didn't."

The Carters were in their mid-forties and prominent business owners in the community. They knew lots of people and were known by many more. Their immediate family was small, but hundreds were employed by their company. Today, an empty seat couldn't be found as the celebration of Bill's all too short life got underway.

The funeral, the week before, was quite different indeed.

Franklin Chester died alone after a long exhausting battle with emphysema. In his final days his breaths were no more than a gasp in and a puff out. For the last eight years he'd fought the battle from Room 302-A of County Nursing Home.

I'd often seen him there when I stopped by to notarize a document or help a family with prearrangements. He was usually shuffling along the hallway in his wheelchair. He used his feet as did so many other residents.

"Hey there Mr. Funeral Guy." He'd say the same thing every time. "How's business. Pretty dead today, eh?" He loved to laugh at his own jokes.

"Yessir. It sure is."

I'd laugh too. Like I always did. Mr. Chester was a good soul. He never seemed to let his meager circumstances or serious health issues bother him. One of those people who made you feel like you mattered. Like he truly cared. I think he did.

As I shook his hand, he pulled me down close to his face. His expression now serious.

"Life looks different if you spend eight years of it in a nursing home." He waved his other arm toward the rooms down the hallway. "I've spent enough time in these places to know."

"Yessir." I smiled back at Mr. Chester. He returned the smile. He seemed grateful for even a little conversation with someone new.

"I'm grateful these places are filled with beautiful and wonderful souls like you, Mr. Chester." I said. "I always see empty faces. So often lonely. It's good they have someone like you to cheer them up on a cloudy day."

Mr. Chester had one nephew who'd come from time to time and check on him. It's not really an unusual thing. Many older folks just don't have anyone left. Sadder is the fact many do have families, but the visits are few and far between.

This was Mr. Chester's story. I learned more about his family when I came to notarize his Power of Attorney.

"Mr. Chester, I assume your nephew is your only living relative?" I said.

"Well, in addition to my nephew, I have had three children." His face wrinkled up. His toothless grin gave him a trusting look. Like the harmless person he was.

"My kids have visited me a total of two times in the last eight years. Twice."

His expression changed from harmless man to distanced dad. We completed the paperwork. He winked. Spun his wheelchair 180 degrees and headed down the hallway. It was the last time I ever saw Frank Chester alive. He died a few months later.

At Mr. Chester's funeral there were eight people: the priest, the organist, the funeral director, the nephew and his wife and a few nurses from the home. None of the children were there. Not one.

Paying your respects at a funeral or memorial service is important. I don't want to minimize it. There is so much more to a life—so much more—than what happens at the end of it.

A human being spends his or her lifetime building thousands of memories which remain with others long after they've died. We all touch many people in many ways along the journey. From birth to death, our stories are worth telling, honoring and remembering.

You may have lost someone close to you and their memorial service was packed with people. Or maybe their funeral ceremony was small with only a few close friends in attendance. It could be there was no ceremony at all. A packed house, slim showing, or lack of ceremony does not reflect the value of a person's life.

No. A life lived is something which happens every moment from birth to death. Whether it's in the sometimes-deceptive trappings of a successful business or in the lonely, quiet halls of a nursing home. The life is no less valued, no less honorable and no less important. Don't ever let anyone tell you otherwise.

Sparks of Life

Whether you're the Queen of England or the humblest person on earth, your life and the lives of those around you matter. Period.

When death touches your life, it seems unreal in many ways. There's just something in us that feels out of place. Strive to let the feeling propel you to not take life for granted.

When you wake up tomorrow, before you even get out of bed, be thankful for the one thing which will set you apart from about 151,000 other people on Earth who didn't.

Some perfect tomorrow values people often overlooked as unimportant. An ancient parable reminds us to treat the rich and influential the same as the poor and obscure. To care for our own family. To know worth comes from far beyond a person's social circumstance. Far beyond.

CHAPTER 24

Hezekiah is a Funny Name

J IM DENNISON WAS DYING. It was stomach cancer. It was hopeless.

Hopeless. The word should be classified an honorary onomatopoeia. Few words carry its weight, fewer still its lamenting tone. Just saying it out loud commands an outer space connection to the awful world. A dark, lifeless planet filled with words like no, never, none, and hopeless. It wouldn't bother his daughter, Christine, if she never heard it again.

Jim was a young 70 years-old when the news hit him like an ill-planned surprise party. No one expected it. The diagnosis stunned his family as it would any other. Cancer. Even with our amazing 21st Century medical technology, the C-Word is often a much too comfortable bedfellow with its ugly cousin, the H Word. Hopeless.

Jim's family was sitting around his bedside one night. It was early in the diagnosis. The mood was filled with hopeful thoughts and heartfelt prayers. Jim could beat this thing. Lots of people do. His youngest daughter, Christine was a praying woman. Not like some of those spooky religious folks on television. No, Christine simply believed God heard her when she talked—and she talked to God a lot.

"You know Dad," she said. She knelt beside the bed. Her young hand holding tightly to his older, rougher, any job to feed my family hand. "I was reading an old story the other day about this guy named Hezekiah. It seems he was dying too. Another guy named Isaiah was a man of faith. He told Hezekiah he was going to live, and God was going to grant him 15 more years of life."

Jim looked at his daughter. His eyes sparkled childlike. He smiled the classic Dennison smile. His large ears raised in the classic Dennison way. Jim also had great faith in this God Christine talked about. From childhood, he'd always found great comfort in the stories in the dusty old Book. Mr. Dennison always treasured the time he and Christine spent talking about heaven, angels, and things too wonderful for humans to wrap their minds around. Yes, Jim had great faith.

"Well Honey," he said. His voice was weaker than Christine would've liked. "I don't see Hezekiah is any different than me."

"Me either, Dad, me either." Christine bowed her head and talked to this God she'd never seen. "God, my dad deserves no less than this Hezekiah dude, so I'm asking you to heal him of this cancer and grant him 15 more years of life. Thank you."

There are millions of stories like this. Some of them end with triumphal and miraculous results where people are genuinely healed from their sicknesses. There are many more which go the other way. Maybe praying isn't as much about asking God for something, like healing your dad from cancer, as it is about giving you something—like the grace and strength you'll need to get through it.

Whatever prayer is for, Christine prayed sincerely, and Jim believed sincerely. The others in the room also nodded their heads in agreement. Everyone said goodnight. It was one of those peaceful moments. When the moment ended, the peace lingered.

The next day Christine called her sister, Gina, and told her what happened the night before. She explained how she really felt God was going to heal their dad and grant him 15 more years. After all, dying at 85 would be much better than dying at 70, right?

Gina also had faith in God. Christine assumed she would be supportive and stand in agreement with her prayer. It's not what happened. After a short and unsolicited big sister lesson about responsible adulthood, Gina lit into her.

"Christine, stop filling Dad's head with fables and fairy tales." Gina said. "You're fostering false hope in Dad and in the rest of the family. You should accept the fact Dad is going to die. Period." Her voice got higher and was cracking. Fewer words between breaths.

Christine could hear Gina's labored breathing on the phone. Gina started crying. Weeping.

"It's okay, Honey," Christine said. "I understand. I know you're hurting like we all are." Her quiet spirit would calm a charging stallion. It was one of Christine's greatest gifts.

Through the years, her positive and childlike faith had taken many near fatal blows from her big sister's hopelessly negative practicality. The sound of Gina's voice suddenly faded into background noise.

In an instant Christine's thoughts momentarily bolted to the old familiar mental and emotional battle. The one she'd fought during a lifetime of struggles with her faith. If hopeful land was a place where dreams come true, this was its dark side. Awful world.

She'd taken more all-expense paid trips to awful world than she cared to remember. It took years of building her faith. Slowly but surely all those negatives which tried their level best to drag her down, turned into positives which propelled her forward.

Hopeful world was where she lived now. She was happier and healthier here. She'd even forgotten the zip code to the other place.

Christine shook her head. Cleared those familiar images of the constant struggle between negative and positive, darkness and light, and gathered her thoughts.

"Gina, I realize Dad could die. I'm not in denial. I just think we can pray for the best. Do whatever we can to make Dad comfortable while remaining confident and optimistic." Christine's voice was kind. You could tell she wasn't going to let Gina's rebuke get her down.

It always puzzled Christine how two sisters raised by the same parents could see things so differently. One remained close, the other distant. One's faith believed all things were possible. The other's faith often seemed to take a back seat to rational pragmatism.

The sisters truly loved each other though. They had genuine faith and there was certainly no doubt they loved their father.

"Ok, Chrissy. I'll see you soon. I love you," Gina said.

"I love you too, Gina."

Christine smiled nostalgic. The corners of her mouth turned up. Her eyes misted. Twinkled. She tilted her head as if listening for a distant sound.

Gina was never much for apologies. Calling her sister, Chrissy was always Gina's way of saying I'm sorry. Christine ended the call and breathed a silent prayer as she hung up. After a pause, and a few cleansing breaths, Christine picked up the phone again and called her dad to see how he was doing.

Six months later, Jim Dennison died.

Fifteen more years of life were not granted. The family was devastated. They'd never lost a father before. Right up until the day he died, Christine believed God was going to heal her dad. She never lost hope.

Her dad also kept his faith and kept loving his family. He'd fought a valiant fight with this dreaded thief of life and lost.

She knew the loss was only physical. He still lived in her heart.

Sparks of Life

There's something magical about hope. Just like Christmas Eve is sometimes more exciting to a child than Christmas Day. When we look forward to a hopeful future our present struggles become more bearable.

Everyone has feelings of hopelessness from time to time. It's one hundred percent human. Being down or depressed is more normal than the pseudo-positive thinkers of the world would have you believe. Go ahead, have your "down times." Just don't stay there. Surround yourself with others who lift you up.

Many of the greatest men and women who've ever lived looked death in the face. All maintained their optimism. They knew life will always triumph over death. You can triumph too. You're just as great as they were.

Some perfect tomorrow is the ultimate outcome of all our hopes. Where small amounts of faith blend with huge expanses of doubt. The result is a power greater than the nuclear energy in the core of our sun. Love.

CHAPTER 25

A Four-Minute Drive

"TRUDY, TRUDY WILLIS," she spelled it out: "W-I-L-L-I-S. She's my good friend and neighbor." This was Mrs. Morgan's answer to my question. "You can call her. My son won't really care when I die. I haven't seen him in years. Just call Trudy."

Mrs. Morgan phoned my office a few days before and asked about prearranging her cremation. I was taking care of another family, so our secretary Carmen Paris took a message. She told her I'd call her back as soon as I was free. When I did, I discovered one of the sweetest, most calming voices I'd ever heard on the other end of the line.

Rose Morgan was 88. She'd let her "fingers do the walking." You'll need to have been born sometime around the 1950s or before to know what that phrase means. She found our number in the Yellow Pages. The printed version. After several exhaustive calls to area funeral homes, she finally found Carmen's kind and reassuring tone to be a breath of fresh air. This convinced her she'd found the right place.

When Mrs. Morgan arrived at the funeral home, Carmen welcomed her and pulled up a chair so they could chat while they waited for me in the arrangement room. This was part of Carmen's special charm. So many of our client families loved her from the start because of her genuineness. After some pleasantries, I explained the process and what we'd be doing over the next hour or so. Mrs. Morgan seemed to relax.

Making funeral prearrangements always begins with gathering some vital statistics. This information is later used to complete the death certificate, so it's imperative this data is accurate, exact and detailed.

"May I have your legal name, please?" I began.

"Rose Marian Morgan," she said. Then, "R-O-S-E M-A-R-I-A-N M-O-R-G-A-N." She sat up straight and proper. Her back never touching the chair. She kept both hands on an unassuming black purse centered in her lap.

I could tell Mrs. Morgan was detail-oriented and would later learn she was a retired elementary school teacher. This explained all the spelling before I had the chance to ask.

The remaining questions were standard: home address, father's name, mother's maiden name, date of birth, Social Security Number, birthplace, etc. When it's a married couple I'm helping, the answer to the next question is assumed to be the spouse. For a single person, it's normally a sibling or an adult child.

For Mrs. Morgan, the next question was visibly painful.

"Who would you like me to list as the Informant? This is usually your legal next-of-kin and the person who will be authorized to take possession of your cremated remains," I explained.

She raised an eyebrow and looked down at her lap. Fiddling with her purse handle, she took a deep breath and moistened her lips. In less than a second, she changed from a sweet, gentle, elderly lady to a distant, troubled, hurting mother.

After an uncomfortable pause, she looked up at me. Her eyes were fixed. Agony was in there. She released her grip on the purse and crossed her arms.

"Trudy, Trudy Willis. My son won't really care when I die. I haven't seen him in years. Just call Trudy." She smiled politely and nodded her head. Her hands returned to the purse in her lap, gently rolling its handle with her thumb and forefinger. She crossed her legs.

In our profession we sometimes experience first-hand the sort of family dynamics many people only see on television reality shows. When a death happens, it's far too common to see families who were barely holding on when life was "normal" sometimes explode. Nothing shakes us like death does.

After Mrs. Morgan's arrangements were all in order and she was on her way back home, I had to do something. My curiosity stirred me to action. I got up the courage, made up my mind, and did the only sensible thing I could imagine.

No, I didn't drive over to her son's house and grab him by the collar. I did go to an online map program to see where he lived in relation to her. Mrs. Morgan's son lived less than a four-minute drive from his mother's house. Four minutes.

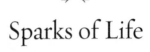

Sparks of Life

Put the book down right this minute.

———

Call the person who came to mind
as you were reading this story.

———

You take it from there.

———

Some perfect tomorrow can be difficult to embrace when important relationships are suffering today. A few relationships may be beyond repair. Leave them alone. Others may only need a nudge. Lots of happy endings start out as nudges.

CHAPTER 26

Smooth Peace

"DON'T THINK FOR A MINUTE YOU'RE going to cremate my mamma." Kyle Jr. wagged his condemning finger inches from his sister's face. His anxious outburst reddened not only his face, but the clenched fist of his other hand.

It was more than just a statement. It was a heartfelt, absolute decree which came from somewhere deep down inside the convictions of this adult son. A son who'd loved his dear mother more than life itself.

The family was seated around the large oval cherry table in the funeral home's arrangement room. The conversation was somber yet pleasant. Kyle's eruption plunged it to a thunderous hush.

If you've ever been in one of those situations when someone says something which shuts every door of response, you'll know what I'm talking about.

The Kneelys were no small family. In addition to Kyle Jr., the son who'd just let his feelings be known, there were four other adult siblings seated at the table this rainy August morning.

They'd lost their dad years ago when his jet was shot down in Vietnam. Kyle, Jr., the youngest of five children, was only three years old back then. Mrs. Kneely never remarried and raised all five children on her own. She was an amazing woman who devoted herself to her children every day of their lives.

Four days ago, she suffered a light stroke but was expected to fully recover. Things took a turn for the worse when she developed a rare type of staph infection in the hospital. Three days later she slipped into an unexpected coma.

She'd never had a cold as far as they knew, let alone a hospital stay. Their mom never recovered. About 7 p.m. the next evening her breathing slowed. Her heart beat one final time, and she died. At 69 years old. Unthinkable for any of the children. Their mom was gone.

Five adult children sat in a funeral home trying to decide what to do. Trying to decide what was right. Trying to decide what Mom would've wanted. In trying to decide, they were painfully discovering none of them really knew for sure.

"Kyle," the youngest sister broke the silence, "we're just talking about our options. No one decided on cremation or not." Cynthia was always the calm one in every family crisis. She looked at Kyle Jr. with her famous "big sissy's got this" face. Her calm hands made a lowering movement. Motioning him to sit back down. A wink signaled her special way of letting him know everything was going to be okay.

"Well, I've made my opinion known," Kyle said. He reached behind him and found the arms of the chair without looking. He took his time sitting back down. His face paled a little back to normal. A few beads of sweat made their way down his temples. "You guys can do whatever you want as long as she's buried and not cremated. Just thinking about it gives me the creeps. I just think it's disrespectful, even barbaric. I know Dad would not have wanted her cremated."

"How in the world can you say something like that, Kyle? You never even knew Dad," one of the other girls shot back at him. "You're not the one in charge here. This is something we all have to agree on." She looked at her other siblings for moral support. She got it. Mostly.

It wasn't hard to tell where this was going. You could feel the tension in the room slowly rising. A few quiet heads were dropped. Eyes looking down at the table. If there'd been blood pressure cuffs on everyone, you'd have seen the numbers rising.

When death touches a family there are so many dynamics present. Even for relatively healthy and loving families, this gripping life event triggers unexpected outcomes. It exposes fault lines never seen and thrusts taboo subjects onto the table.

"Let me say something," the other brother interrupted. "I think cremation is the smart thing to do. It's good for the environment, it's a lot cheaper and I think it's easier on the family not having to see…" He swallowed hard and bit his lip. You could tell he was holding it back—the lump in his throat came out of nowhere.

The funeral director sat quietly for the next few minutes and let them talk amongst themselves. Slowly he stood up.

"I have a few things to take care of and some forms I'll need you to sign. Why don't you all just talk about what you'd like to do, and I'll be back in a few minutes," he said.

He offered the family a kind-hearted glance on his way out of the room. He saw this played out so many times before. The names changed, the ages varied, the number of family members around the table fluctuated, but this particular scenario happened more than most people knew.

Another good family whose lives were suddenly turned upside-down was trying to figure out the "right thing" to do when making final arrangements. It wasn't ever about who was right or wrong. There's no right or wrong when it comes to these decisions.

Their mother never talked with a friend or a funeral planner to make her wishes known. The funeral director knew these adult children would never be able to answer two questions. Did we do the right thing? Did we do what Mom would've wanted?

Even though they knew their mom so well, like most children they'd never talked to her about this. She'd never brought the subject up. They were too busy living to think about dying.

After 15 minutes the funeral director walked back into the arrangement room. There were only three children seated. Kyle had stormed out of the building and his big sister had run out after him. The room was heavy. An uncomfortable atmosphere hung around the table.

It would take a long time to come to grips with the choices they'd been forced into making today. What they would do with their mother's mortal remains. This most loving of women. The one who gave them their lives.

Kyle and his sister came through the door and slowly made their way back to their seats. He'd been crying. She'd been crying. They both looked exhausted. Kyle appeared drained.

"Whatever they want I'll go along with," he said. He looked at the funeral director. His head lowered. It remained still while his eyes glanced around the table.

The sister spoke up. "I need to say something," she said. "We all know dad's remains were never recovered in Vietnam. Even though we've never talked too much about it, it's always bothered me." She looked at the funeral director and then at Kyle Jr. "Whether we cremate mom or not, I don't want her to end up scattered in some river or buried in some cold, dark cemetery all by herself."

The words barely out of her mouth, she broke down. Sobs came freely. Unhindered. A few siblings immediately stood up came to her side. Big sissy, who was never far from a tissue, offered her a box of them. She patted her back with her older, steady hand. This calmed her sister a little. She sat down quietly, not really sure where her statement would fit into the rest of the conversation.

The funeral director scanned the faces around the arrangement room table. Cynthia and Kyle Jr. were still settling back into their chairs.

"Is there a government marker placed in your dad's memory in Arlington or any other national cemetery?" he said. "I'd have to do some research but if there is, there's a very good chance a place may have been reserved for your mom next to his grave. A veteran's spouse may also be buried in a national cemetery, whether in a casket or in the form of cremated remains."

"Yes." The oldest sister blurted. Her eyes flashed with a hint of excitement. She smacked her hand on the table. A small triumph. Her next words were brighter, almost jovial. "I hadn't thought about this. When I was little, we'd visit his grave in

Arlington on our trips up to Philadelphia. We stopped going as much when Aunt Joan died because we didn't get up north much anymore. I had no idea Mom could be buried there too."

A few distant smiles struggled to the surface for the first time all day. Almost magically, a smooth peace seemed to fill the room. It was like someone finally turned on a tiny light in a hopelessly darkened room. The siblings all looked at each other. For the first time, they felt like something concrete had been decided. The difficult day would end after all.

Kyle got up and walked over to the sister who went outside with him. He bent down and gave her a heartfelt hug. Almost on cue, the others followed suit. The next few moments, this family racked with pain and surprise and doubt and anger and uncertainty, lovingly held each other as only siblings who've lost a parent can.

They still had a long way to go and many decisions to make. One was still the original question. Burial or cremation? Thanks to the funeral director's wise guidance, at least they had a sense of unity they'd not had before.

At this exact moment, peace gently put its hand on each child's shoulder. It then gracefully stepped away, found a seat in the corner and waited patiently. It would be needed again many more times before the day was over.

Sparks of Life

Nobody is ever truly ready for what happens when someone dies. There's no formula for grieving, no universal template—each walks his own path. There's no guarantee we'll all live to the ripe old age we envision.

Giving thought ahead of time to what type of arrangements you would want when you die takes a great burden from those who are left behind.

It's not morbid to talk about dying and what is to be done with your body. On the contrary not talking about it is much worse. Think about what your family would be doing if it were you who had died and make some plans.

Some perfect tomorrow doesn't favor the visionary over the rational thinker. Hoping for a better world melds closely with managing the one we have now. Your peace of mind is enhanced by helping the ones you love. Peace of mind. Aim there.

CHAPTER 27

Whose Funeral?

"**D**EATH COMES UNEXPECTEDLY." The baritone thundered.

On the platform the pulpit vibrated. The chandeliers on the ceiling shook. In the pews the congregants sat muscles tensed. On their faces, expressions waxed in fear.

I borrowed this scene from Disney's 1960 screen production of Eleanor Porter's 1913 novel, Pollyanna. If you're not familiar with the story, Pollyanna conquered the small town of Harrington by spreading her contagious optimistic sunshine to many of the sourpusses who lived there. In this scene, Sunday churchgoers were accosted by this opening line in the pastor's sermon: "Death comes unexpectedly."

If you've not seen this movie, I would highly recommend it. In our day of high-tech motion picture special effects, all-too-often mixed with a weak plot (if a plot at all), a 1960s Disney film is always a reminder of what is good and right with the world—while still capturing its shortcomings in parody.

To view this scene on the big screen and to see it happen in real life—in person, at a funeral—are different experiences altogether. I'd watch Pollyanna over and over again. I hope I never again experience this next story—for as long as I live.

The funeral chapel was rather small. I would guess no more than 80 strangers or maybe 100 close friends could've fit in its pews. The casket was placed as usual directly in front of the pulpit. It was half-opened at the left end, revealing only the departed loved one's upper torso. His hands were clasped left over right, head turned ever so slightly to the right. He wore his best—and his last suit.

The background music stopped as the service started precisely at 11 a.m. A classic funeral time of day. The sharply clad speaker approached the pulpit. His tailored charcoal suit accessorized with a large black Bible. Which he kept tucked under his left arm. Heels clicked. Like tap shoes. In perfect time on the hardwood floor.

He took the stage and stood erect. Proper. Dignified. Not a hair out of place. He asked everyone to close their eyes and bow their heads for the opening prayer. His prayer began softly and reverently.

"Dear God, we ask grace and comfort for the family. We ask you to usher this loved one into your arms." He cleared his throat. "Grant your grace O, God, we ask. Amen"

This is a pretty standard opening prayer for religious funerals. This was where anything which could be labeled standard ended. Abruptly.

I have attended literally thousands of funeral services. You'd think I'd be ready for almost anything. People are different. Families are different. Funeral services should be different, right? Uh, right.

It was as if this preacher had some sort of NASCAR motor revving up inside of him. It cranked up at the opening prayer, idled smoothly while reading the obituary, and gradually increased speed coming out of the pits while he quoted a few Bible verses. Then, before anyone knew it, we were careening at 212 MPH with Bill Elliot in his 1987 qualifying run at Talladega. Preacher at the wheel.

Yes, we all get excited when we talk about something we're passionate about. I do. You do. We all do. It's just human nature and there's nothing at all wrong with it. It's one of the cool things about humans.

But imagine a golf commentator using a whispery voice while calling play-by-play at a college football game. There's going to be some disconnect there. Something just doesn't seem to fit. It's how it felt at this funeral service. Only swap the whispering golf guy for his football-shoutin' cousin commentating on the 18th green at the PGA championship.

It wasn't the preacher was merely screaming. Which he was. Or he was unsure of his passion. Which he wasn't. Or he'd missed his calling as a radio sports announcer. Which he had. Or he'd failed an assertive speaking course in college. Which he hadn't.

It's in almost 45 minutes, yes, forty-five, of ranting and raving he did something I personally feel is a monumental failure at a funeral. He neglected to even once mention the name of the man who was lying in the casket. You know, the person whose life brought us all together today? Yeah, him.

In 45 minutes, he didn't speak of his life, his family, his loves, his career, or even his favorite hobby. Nor, remarkably, even his name. Not once. We had no more idea who this guy in the casket was after the service ended, than before it started. It's one of the saddest things I've ever seen.

Yes, it's important folks who gather to honor a life lived consider and ponder the brevity of their own lives. It's also important to take time to do some serious thinking about how we're living it. To think what changes could be made before we're the one lying in a casket or filling an urn with our ashes.

This preacher took advantage of helpless people. Sitting on uncomfortable benches some place they'd rather not be. He used the opportunity solely as a bully pulpit.

I've been to some funerals where, after I left, I felt more at peace with the world, at home in my own skin and in love with this wonderful, beautiful creation we all take for granted. These ceremonies truly honored the person's life. I went away feeling like mine really mattered.

I've been to at least one which made me want to apologize for being human.

"Death comes unexpectedly," is a great idea to make us think more about life. Few of us are truly changed and challenged by someone yelling at us about anything.

Maybe the preacher could have lunch with Pollyanna before his next church parishioner dies.

Sparks of Life

This is somewhat of a comical story. If you weren't there. Life exists in both tragedy and comedy. Give some thought to whom you trust—not only the ones who stand up and officiate ceremonies like this, but the ones you walk with every day.

If ever you've been to a funeral service like I described, there's only one thing to do. Be glad it's over. While we're at it, pray for and be kind to the preacher who thinks he's a NASCAR driver.

One of the most important things you can do is sit down and record on paper or computer how you'd like your own celebration of life to be. Let your family know the person you'd like to have as speaker—and then call the person to discuss it. Tell them to talk about you. Make sure your local funeral home or cremation provider has this information on record as well.

Some perfect tomorrow holds honor in high regard. When we honor another, we honor ourselves. Our community. Our world. You can honor someone without fanfare. Without a viral video. Without an event at all. In your heart.

CHAPTER 28

Nine Hundred Dollars

"**M**R. SEATON?"

The caller's voice on the cell phone was weak and distant.

"Yes?" I answered.

"My mother just died. I was referred to you by a mutual friend. She said you could help me." He sniffed, cleared his throat and took a deep breath. "We didn't think it was going to be this quick. I just don't know what to do."

"I'm so sorry about your mother. How can I help you?"

"Well, I've never been through this before and I need to know what my next step is."

"Where is your mother now?"

"In the hospital."

"When did she die?"

"This morning at 9:17."

If you're a plumber, you get used to people stuffing something down their drains, clogging up the whole system.

If you're an electrician, your service call volume around Christmastime must be doubled with customers trying to get the most out of their allotted household amperage.

If you're a successful bankruptcy attorney, it doesn't surprise you when someone walks in your office and tells you they can't pay their bills.

Why is it, if you're a funeral professional like me, you never seem to quite understand this kind of call? It's not someone has died. No, we are here for the families we serve. Same as plumbers, electricians and lawyers are there for their clients. It's what often comes after the "someone has died" part.

Reading this short dialogue, you must think this sounds normal. Someone dies. The family calls a funeral home. The funeral home asks some questions and lets them know what to do. You would be right. This is exactly what we do. Why we're here. Our profession.

This particular phone call was not to the funeral home though. I was on my way home from the office and my cell phone rang. As a successful funeral professional, many people refer me to anyone who may need my services.

I am not a funeral director. I'm a preneed funeral planner. I do some of the same things a funeral director does: arranging the service, gathering vital statistics, helping with selection of a casket or an urn, and many other details. My job is to do this while someone is still living.

When I get a call like this, I let the person know what I do, and will answer any questions they have. All they know is I am the "funeral guy" and someone they trust recommended they call me. I tell them they'll need to meet with a licensed funeral director to make the arrangements since the death already occurred. I let them know what to expect. What the timeline is. What they need to do now. This puts them at ease.

Death is not something all of us face every day of our lives. Most of us may have to make final arrangements for someone three, maybe four times in our entire lives. Some will make more, some less.

This particular mother was 77 years old. Today, she left behind: three adult children, five young-adult grandchildren, a brother and two sisters, and several nieces and nephews. Unlike many families today, all her family still lived within ten miles of each other.

This mother had no life insurance. No savings. No plan. This particular mother never thought she was going to die.

The family said they didn't know how they were going to come up with the $900 for a simple cremation. Nine hundred dollars. There are some who genuinely live on such meager means this amount of money may as well be a million dollars. There are others who simply don't care.

Most of us live somewhere between those two extremes. We all place value on what we regard as worthy. We take care of the things important to us. We place enormous amounts of money and effort into things which, in the end, make little difference.

Think about it. A human life is worth honoring. A human body is worth honoring after the life has gone out of it.

My wife and I were walking after dinner just the other night and there was a little dead squirrel in the middle of the road. I picked it up and moved it over in the grass on the roadside. Honor. Honoring a person who's died doesn't mean you have to spend $25,000 on a casket like Michael Jackson's.

These decisions must be made when death occurs. They take a toll on everyone involved. The ones who've had the forethought to plan their own final arrangements in advance take this burden from the ones they will leave behind.

This family did come up with the funds to take care of their mother's body after all. They turned out to be one of the sweetest families I've ever known. One of the adult children called me several months after her mom's death. She had questions about how she could make some of these hard decisions for herself today to help her family tomorrow.

Sparks of Life

Stories like this one are more common than you may think. People walk unnecessarily unprepared through the doors of funeral homes and cremation providers every day.

Whether cremation or burial would be your choice, making these decisions in advance is important. No less important than all the other life planning things you do.

How good you'll feel to have your final arrangements prearranged. Bucket List? Most likely not. Whatever list you use, it'll be a gift of love one day.

Some perfect tomorrow does not eclipse reality. It provides hope when reality doesn't look all that perfect. Right now. In what you're going through today. It can help you. Give you hope. Priceless hope.

CHAPTER 29

Dad's Gone

THE CALL CAME AT 2:30 IN THE MORNING.
I knew it would come. I thought I was prepared. I thought I knew how I'd react. I thought I could handle this. Thoughts can be deceptive. They can fool you. Thoughts can be thinly veiled suits of armor. All of mine turned out to be nothing but smoke. Some protection they were. Thanks thoughts.

"Dad's gone," breathed my brother's voice on phone. There was strength in his words.

"I know," I said. "Were you with him?"

"Yes."

"How's Mom?"

"She's okay. She's tired."

"I'll be there as soon as I can tomorrow. I love you."

"I know you do. Craig?"

"Yeah, Matt?"

"I'm so glad you're my brother."

"Me too, Matt. I love you, man."

"I love you too."

As I hung up the phone, I sat there on the edge of the bed for a few minutes. My wife, Tami was awakened by the call. She knew what it was. There was little need to tell her but getting it out seemed to help.

"He's gone." I somehow managed to get the words out. The tears came right after. Throat stiffened. Nose stuffed. I felt a warm hand on my back as she scooted over to my side of the bed. It's amazing—the power of touch.

There were thousands of words in her touch. Not one of them could've outdone the sheer power in those fingers as she rubbed them lightly across my shoulders.

I got up and stood beside the bed for a second. I knew going back to sleep wasn't an option. "I'm going out to the living room for a while," I said.

"Need me to come out there with you?" she whispered.

"No, I'll be okay."

She understood. Twenty-five years earlier it was her dad. Yes, she understood all too well.

The couch welcomed me like an old friend. I sank down into it for a moment and then sat forward, wrapping my arms around my knees. Relaxing didn't feel right. Funny how there's purpose even in posture sometimes.

The house was still and dark. It seemed to know I needed stillness and darkness.

There are times in your life which stand out from the rest. Stand taller than other times. So many years later—this one still towers over many.

My dad lost a brief battle with pancreatic cancer. It seems this is one of the worst kinds of cancer since it sometimes veils itself behind the complex of organs near the pancreas. He was diagnosed in March and didn't even see the end of September.

Having never yet lost a parent, I really didn't know how I'd react. I thought I'd be strong. I was for everyone else. I was strong from the initial shock of the news. To the futile treatments. Right up through to the hopeless surgery.

It was one of those surgeries when the doctor comes out with "that look" on his face. God bless doctors for having to make the look—followed closely by the words—words they use to tell hopeful families their hope fell short of its goal. Thanks Docs.

Months later, the night the call came, it was the couch which let me know my strength had finally come to its end. I guess couches have a way of doing that—especially the 3 o'clock in the morning kind. Thanks Couch.

I'm not sure how many groans originate in the soles of feet, but this one did. It began in the farthest possible location away from my mouth. The absolute other end of my body. If its birth could have been measured, the meter would've registered the layer of skin on the bottom of my feet as its starting point.

Before it reached my other end, it seemed to vibrate and encompass everything in its path, ankles, knees, hips. When it got above the hips, it stopped to build up steam in my stomach. It stayed there for the longest time.

Then, it churned its way up through my torso, downgrading a violent vomit to a child's toy. A vomit would've been manageable, predictable. I would've traded in this feeling for a dozen vomits. When this energy reached its zenith, it poured out of me a bursting dam. Though I'd felt it coming since the tingle of my feet only seconds ago, it still surprised me when it became audible.

To say I cried would equate this phenomenon with a sneeze or a cough. This was no mere cry. This was the death of my father ravaging the fundamental center of my being. It hurt. It stung. It squeezed. It overwhelmed me and left me breathless. It just kept washing over me like ocean waves. I didn't think it would ever end.

It's funny. All these words I have at my disposal. Tens of thousands of them—and the ones I've just chosen to describe this experience fall pale and hopelessly short. It was grief.

They say you grieve in proportion to how much you love. I guess I loved my dad a lot. It would be almost 12 years before the groan came back for its second visit—but losing Mom is a whole other story.

Sparks of Life

When someone's no longer in our lives, it can affect us in some strange ways. Some ways are almost "normal." Others break into our lives like a night-covered burglar.

There's healing in grief. It may not seem like it at the moment, but there will come a refreshing. You may feel worse before you feel better.

Crying is normal. Crying is vital. Crying is human.

Some perfect tomorrow is well acquainted with grief. Love itself forms the perfect center of—and extreme borders of—grief. Grieving travels where it may, but it can never escape love. Nor exist apart from it.

CHAPTER 30

Pouting Less

"GOOD MORNING MY DARLING SON. I just wanted to tell you I think maybe the little blue pill might be working. I know God's working. I-think-I'm-going-to-make-it, Baby. I love you. You don't need to call me back. I know you've got a busy day, but your mama loves you. Bye, Baby."

A verbatim transcript of one of my mother's final (recorded) messages to me. In her very next voicemail, like a mother with her young child sitting on her lap, she was reciting a verse of scripture and asking me if I could finish it. "This is the day the LORD has made..." This mother was 82 and her young child was 52.

Electronically anyway, there are few things in my life I am more grateful for than these saved voicemails. She left them on my cellphone during the last few months of her life on Earth.

Mom called most every morning to give me my "morning wake-up call." On several of those mornings she'd call about the time I was shaving. Rather than answer, for some cosmic reason I'd let my phone go to voicemail and call her back on my way into the office. Retrospectively, this seemingly insignificant act was purposed. Maybe even providential. I have those treasured recordings and can listen to them anytime I want. Somehow, hearing her voice, even in this artificial way, gives me great comfort.

Mom was in a nursing home for a few months for rehabilitation. She fell and developed some other symptoms which required intense physical and occupational therapy. As with many elderly patients, especially women, she'd developed a urinary tract infection (UTI) during her stay there. This greatly affected her reasoning for several days while the doctors tried to get it under control.

For any adult child who's been through this particular saga, you know how challenging it can be. Along with lethargy and irritation, this type of infection can sometimes trigger symptoms of delirium in older women. With my mom, this was the case.

Almost overnight, Mom went from her normal bubbly and hopeful self, to being absolutely "out of it." She didn't seem to recognize us. She would only stare blankly into space while occasionally uttering a word or two.

I remember one time I was frustrated. A little upset with her for not talking to me. Yet to realize the UTI was causing the delirium. I said something like, "Mom, I'm just going to sit here until you answer me."

She bent forward. Her hands surprised me as they took mine. I didn't expect her to react physically. I sat up straight and focused on her eyes. I wanted to see Mom again, if only for a moment. A little color returned to her cheeks. She blinked a few times and sighed. The consummate caring mother, she left the empty stare, looked me in the eye and replied with a one-word sentence: "Pouting."

Her eyes sparkled as only mothers' eyes can. She smiled her sweet smile. Releasing my hands, she relaxed in her chair. Caring hands returned to her lap. The stare then returned.

To her, in the briefest of moments, I was a stubborn child (50 years removed), and she was lovingly correcting my behavior. It remains another precious memory. It's funny how incidents which were at the time frustrating, even painful, can blossom into private smile-makers later in life.

To my mother's credit, she always maintained her sweet and loving demeanor—even while battling the disrupting effects of this infection. The "little blue pill" she mentioned in the voice-mail was her way of saying, "I'm feeling more like myself every day." As she was coming out of the infection thanks to some high-power antibiotics, the doctor had prescribed something like a low-grade valium to make her feel more herself—thus the "little blue pill."

Mom was in the nursing home until her death several months later. This was an emotionally painful time for all of us. The ensuing grief shattered my family.

Years later, I am just beginning to see these events from a higher perspective. No, I've not "gotten over" her death, as many a well-wishing (but badly-mistaken) friend would suggest—but I did get through it. I am learning to embrace those moments which surrounded her final months of life.

I think I'm even beginning to cherish her death, as strange as it may sound. I often turn it over in my mind, not to relive the hurt, but to examine it and see what it holds for me now. In this moment. As I do, an odd kind of peace takes up a little more space in my heart than before. I'm not getting over it. I probably never will, but I'm pouting less.

Sparks of Life

Right in the middle of the pain, you can know there's a bright ray of hope being formed even now. You may not see it for quite some time, but just knowing it's there will help.

You may not have saved voice messages or other recorded treasures but look around. There's a storehouse of rich and soothing memories you carry with you wherever you go.

Take a few minutes and think about the memories you'll leave for those who survive you. Make a purposed effort to leave more good ones than bad. Like Hansel's and Gretel's path of breadcrumbs in the forest, you'll deposit true wealth for them to inherit no silly bank account could possibly hold.

Some perfect tomorrow is brimming with goodness. Goodness in life results from good remembrances. It is both created and embraced. Self-sustaining. Go create some goodness.

CHAPTER 31

Eight Fifty-Two

A S SOON AS THE STRETCHER CLEARED the back of the ambulance, I somehow knew she was already gone.

Inside me, hope was cheering the paramedics on as they worked their magic, but something deep within was already trying to resolve the unresolvable. I would never again hear my mother's voice, see her smile or feel her amazing hugs. Years later the image still makes me cry.

It was Saturday morning. Sleeping in day. Who on Earth would call me before 8 a.m. on a Saturday? I lazily let the call go to voicemail so I could decide if it was important. Half-eyed, I turned over to the nightstand and saw the caller ID was the Nursing Home.

Thinking Mom had left a message for my "morning wake-up call," I pressed the green button. I prepared to hear her sweet, soft voice say something like, "Good morning Sugar...."

The voice was anything but sweet and she didn't call me Sugar.

"Mr. Seaton, this is Angela at the rehab center. I wanted to let you know your mother was short of breath and her skin was slightly clammy, so we called for an ambulance to take her to the hospital."

Mom had been short of breath before and, besides, since the voice from the nursing home didn't have a pressing sense of urgency, I drove normally on the 10-minute trip to the hospital. When I arrived, I went immediately to the information desk and learned Mom's ambulance was still on the way. I had time to slip over to the hospital coffee shop for a cup of black morning wake-up. There was little need to rush. I trusted the professionals at the nursing home and well-trained first responders in the ambulance were doing their jobs.

As I made my way back across the parking lot the ambulance pulled in. I stood at a distance, giving the paramedics berth. They didn't need my help. I positioned myself so I could be the welcomed and cheerful face Mom would need to see when she cleared the opened back doors of the vehicle. She didn't see me.

In my mind I think I heard the movie director yell into his megaphone, "Action!" It was as if I was suddenly watching a motion picture. Surreal. Separate. Distant. I stood. Coffee in hand, watching this short film about an elderly lady being rolled across a hospital parking lot on a gurney.

The actors in the film were smooth and professional. They obviously rehearsed their parts hundreds of times. I was amazed how the lady playing the part of the patient on the stretcher remained so still while the other actors performed very real-looking CPR on her all the way through the emergency room doors.

Fantasy quickly gave way to reality as I came out of my momentary trance and followed the stretcher crew. This was no leading lady and her supporting actors, but my own mother and her emergency caregivers darting for those foreboding glass doors with the huge word "Emergency" emblazoned in red. It was really Mom. She was really still.

I spent the next 20 minutes or so in the hallway right outside Trauma Room #1. Sometimes pacing. Standing. Sitting on the floor with knees drawn up and held by now-weakening arms. I'd long forgotten about the cup of coffee. It ended up in the trashcan right outside the glass doors only a sip or two from full.

Thinking back on those moments, I now understand when someone experiences an unbelievable event like this and says, "I'm not sure what just happened. It was all so fast...."

"I'm calling it zero-eight-fifty-two." The strong yet gentle female voice broke above the confusing symphony of electronic beeps. Shuffling feet and medical terms were tossed back and forth. I'd listened through the thin curtain which separated Trauma Room #1 from Traumatized Son #2.

I guess I'd watched too many television trauma dramas to doubt why the strong voice called out the exact time in military format. At eight minutes 'til nine in the morning that day my mother's spirit had "officially" left her body. She was gone.

When the owner of the female voice stepped from behind the curtain, I was already on my feet. Her eyes met mine and revealed an angst her lab coat couldn't soften.

I knew she knew I knew. I found myself almost trying to console her and show her kindness while she inhaled deeply to power her next words. I doubt any amount of medical schooling taught her how to say them.

"Are you her son?"

"Yes."

"I'm so sorry," she said. "Your mom didn't make it." She straightened the stethoscope around her neck. Empty hands looked for some place to go. They settled in her oversized coat pockets for a second. Gentle eyebrows stressed a caring face. She pursed her upper lip.

There was a comfortable, uncomfortable pause.

"I know. Thank you for trying. Can I see her?"

"Yes," she said. Her gentle eyebrows straightened to a firm look. She extended a firmer two-handed handshake which let me know they'd tried their best and done all they could.

"The nurse will be out in a moment. I'm so sorry."

She gave a polite smile and turned to go down the hall. Her heels reverberated on the highly polished hospital floor. Her shoulders relaxed a little as she walked. She tilted her head from side to side, stretching her neck. Her footsteps joined the background noise.

I took a deep breath. The nurse pulled back the curtain.

If you've ever been to the Saturday Matinee featuring the mental movie I just shared, you'll know the dreamlike lingering memories which lodge themselves like uninvited houseguests in your mind.

Death presents itself in many forms. Sometimes, like when you're facing a loved one's terminal illness, it shows itself as an ominous specter lying in wait. Always just around the next corner. Other times it sneaks up on you. It sucks all the air out of your lungs right between breaths.

When you're the first human being to know death just happened to someone you love, let's just say it is indescribable.

You're the first to see them not breathing anymore. The first who gets to let it start "sinking in." The first to do one of the hardest, yet surprisingly, most cleansing of tasks. You must then inform the second human being someone they loved just died.

There's something about sharing our fearful and dreadful thoughts, which become words, with another person. It lets us know we're not the only one on the planet who will have to face this.

Sparks of Life

Memories like these can haunt us if we let them. Don't. They can help us heal if we let them. Do.

———

Few things can shake us to our very hearts like traumatic events. Let it remind you of the brevity and fragility of life. Vow to embrace the loved ones near you even more. Embracing is good.

———

No matter the circumstances of your loved one's death, there are little moments known only to you which can strengthen, even embolden you as you keep walking on. Walking on is good. Walking on is living.

———

Some perfect tomorrow will wrap you with folds of understanding in tragedy. In loss. Heartbreak. Surprise. In the life events beyond our ability to grasp. Hold onto hope. There comes a time when current pain will ease off. A little. Then a little more.

CHAPTER 32

Aprons and Hugs

MY GRANDMOTHER'S BODY looked like a wax dummy. Lying in a long weird-looking box. She wasn't moving—at all—the stillest grandma ever. This was the first funeral I'd ever attended. The first person I'd ever seen who wasn't alive. It may have been at this very moment something inside me changed, if only slightly—something I would only realize years later.

We all look back on our firsts: first kiss, first love, first car, first date, first dance.

First death.

The first death I experienced was the person whose love for me was second only to my mom's. This was Grandma Baker. My Grandma Baker. My mom's mother.

Now she was gone. Seeing her motionless in her coffin that day, my stomach churned. Heart pounded. I felt out of breath. Like I'd run a mile. It had a palpable, powerful effect on me back then. It still does today.

I was a normal rebellious middle child. I gave my parents their fair share of gray hairs. Growing up in the 1960s and 70s,

I certainly had my share of rebellious role models—whom I tried my best to emulate. It's not I didn't care. It's just most of the care was directed at the boy who looked back at me in the mirror every day.

I was popular, lots of friends, lots of curly hair and lots of life. Deep inside I could be selfish. No one ever depended on me for anything. Today the selfish part of my life would end abruptly. For the first time in my life, someone would need me more than I needed them. This someone was my mom.

I had to be the first to the funeral home that day. Maybe it was simple curiosity. Or maybe some unrevealed preparation for a call of duty to help the mother who raised me, prepare to bury the mother who raised her.

The viewing was to begin at 5 o'clock that evening, but Grandma was already "laid out" a little after noon. The place was empty, except for the long box at the end of the room. I knew it held the body of this special lady. The lady who'd fried more chicken, worn more aprons, and given more hugs than anyone I'd ever known. All in classic grandmother style.

I couldn't go up to the coffin for a long time. There was a chair in the back of the parlor. I sat there. The distance was safe. The view was surreal. The music was a recording of some guy playing a spooky, sad pipe organ.

I finally found the courage to stand up and walk toward the coffin. Slowly, reverently, I made my way to my grandma's body. As I got closer I remember a sick feeling in my gut. The kind you get when you're standing close to the edge of a very high cliff. Your brain takes great pleasure in letting you know for a split-second what it might feel like if you leaned out just a bit more.

I didn't cry for a long time. I was in a dream and this wasn't real. Wax dummy. Spooky organ music. Dead person in a long box.

A cry made its way out. It tumbled me like a big ocean wave. Knocked me over. Unmercifully held me underwater. It hurt. It stayed. Left as suddenly as it came.

Right up until a few hours later. When I met my mom at the funeral home door. Until I tried hard not to look her in the eye. When I held out my arm for Mom to grab onto. Until her knees buckled when we turned the corner and she caught sight of the coffin for the first time.

When she realized her mother was not going to recover from the cancer which ate away at her life for the last year. Until she looked at the face that had always looked back at hers. It wasn't looking back today. She knew it never would again. Right up until that time.

The cry that gushed out of me earlier miraculously behaved itself and stayed inside. It remained in my throat just below the Adam's Apple. The cry stayed in because now, I had a greater immediate calling than to mourn my grandmother's death. My mother needed me now. I could mourn later.

Many years and many, many funerals later, I know that day was preparing me for what I would ultimately do as part of my life calling. Helping someone through a death somehow helps the helper through life.

Sparks of Life

There's no way of truly knowing why we go through the things life throws our way, but almost always in retrospect, we see there was purpose in the pain.

If there are people in your life who helped you through your loss, realize they are hurting too. Take some time to comfort them. No matter how hard it might seem right now.

For some reason we've been destined to be involved in the life of someone touched by death. You are the only person on earth who can help them like you can. They need you. You may not realize it, but you need them too.

Some perfect tomorrow survives in exact proportion to personal empathy. Without empathy you cannot thrive. Exist, yes. Thrive, no. By understanding what others go through we shorten the gap between us. We also benefit personally. We're better prepared to experience future loss. Future life. With understanding. Thriving.

CHAPTER 33

Only Moments

"YOU SEE THAT PICTURE RIGHT THERE?" Whispered the unmistakable Missouri accent behind me. "That was you when you were just 4 years-old. Right after your mama took that picture, the three of us headed down to the lake. It was your first fishing trip. We fished all afternoon and didn't get so much as a nibble, but you had a ball. Your daddy was so proud of you. I remember you said the worms felt 'squishy'. That's your daddy's smile you got smeared all over your face, you know."

Uncle Joe had a way of taking something as simple as an old photograph and making it come to life. Lots of old photos were coming to life this evening.

We all gathered in the funeral home chapel. The photos were projected one by one on the overhead screen. The screen was positioned directly above the casket containing the body of my dear father.

The last sentence may make you sad. Not too many folks like the idea of a body lying in a casket. The body in the casket is not what this story is about.

"Hey Jimmy, there's you and Mama at our old house down near the sand mines."

Charlie slapped Jimmy on the back in a way only Charlie could get away with. As Uncle Jimmy recovered, I looked up at the projected faded photo of him and his dear mother. I'd never seen Grandma Seaton without her apron on.

"And you." Charlie said. Continuing the ribbing. "You're wearing that goofy old hat. I used to think you slept in that stinky thing."

Jimmy just smiled his famous smile my dad always said reminded him of Clark Gable. Like Uncle Joe, Jimmy was one of the sweetest and kindest men I knew. He and his wife Allene couldn't have children of their own. When I was a boy, I always thought it was odd. Didn't everybody have children? Uncle Jimmy and Aunt Allene treated my siblings and me like we were their very own. There's a blessing everywhere if you look hard enough.

My brother, sister and I loved visiting their old wooden house outside of town. They always had a special present for us under the tree at Christmastime.

Charlie immediately flew in from San Juan when he got the news about Dad. Still as thin and tanned as ever, we always thought he was the "cool" uncle. Most of my dad's siblings were artists but Charlie seemed to create more than the rest. I still have some of his paint brushes which I treasure.

Like Dad, Charlie would always have way too many pens in his top pocket. I never saw him wearing anything except one of his guayabera shirts from Puerto Rico. Most people know these as Mexican Wedding shirts or Yucatan Shirts, but to us there was only one name for them. Uncle Charlie shirts.

While I was watching Charlie and Jimmy joke around, I felt a soft hand patting me on the back. I knew it was Esther before I even turned around.

"Hey there young fella," she said. Her deep green eyes hid behind classic 1950s horn rimmed glasses. She kept patting my back the whole time. Speaking in her typical matter of fact fashion.

If you didn't know Aunt Esther, by her tone of voice you may think she was mad at you. Nothing could be further from the truth. She was a loving sister and the one closest to Dad. He always looked up to her with great respect and love.

Esther was never shy of letting the world know her opinions. She didn't mind telling you what she thought about a subject. Whether you wanted to hear it or not.

"Hello Aunt Esther. You doin' alright?" I said. I knew the answer in advance.

"Yeah, honey I'm just fine. I'm so sorry about your daddy. He was a good man. I gave your dad a bunch of my African violets a few years back."

She waved her hand in a crossing motion. As if she was presenting her award-winning flowers to the judges. Her eyes widened. Her hand returned to patting me on the back.

"He treated those plants just like they were his babies. I remember he loved to try out his new-fangled video camera on them. He must've burned up a thousand feet of film—uh, if those contraptions even use film anymore."

Childhood memories of Aunt Esther's house flooded my mind. African Violets by the dozen lined the shelves on her screened-in porch. The piano and organ in her music room.

After the Beatles came to America in 1964, I developed my interest in music. Aunt Esther's spinet piano and Hammond organ played a big part in my instrument of choice. Our house was quite a bit smaller than hers. How cool was it to have an entire room in your house dedicated to nothing but music?

Silently, Grandma and Granddaddy sat over near the wall watching the photos scroll across the big screen, listening to the stories, soaking it all in. I knew they were sad my dad was gone, but somehow, they kept from crying.

Their grief must've been soothed to some degree by the surreal scene playing out before them. All their children were in one place. The last time they were all together was years ago. Captured in one of those black and white images projected on the screen.

In one photo, all the ladies wore long skirts and bobbed hair. The men were all in white shirt sleeves, pants pulled way up above their waistlines. It was the fashion of the day. The running board of a 1932 Ford sedan provided a footrest for a few of the fellas. Grandma Seaton had her apron on.

I was barely into my conversation with Aunt Esther when Elizabeth walked through the door. I'd always thought she looked the most like Grandma. I half expected to see an apron tied around her waist. She had one of those infectious Mona Lisa smiles. She and her husband operated a small grocery store in a town a few miles away. She always encouraged my music.

"Well, hey there Mr. Music Man." Aunt Elizabeth's eyes closed so tightly when she smiled it was a wonder she could even see. Her entire face beamed when she smiled. She was wearing the same perfume I remembered as a child. The super sweet fragrance would take your breath away if you got a good whiff. Your nose always knew when Aunt Elizabeth was in the room.

"Ain't you just a sight to be seen standin' around with all these old fogies?" She quickly shooed everyone else away so she could get in a proper hug. "Your daddy was so proud of you and your brother and sister. He still is, you know."

"Yes ma'am." I answered. I always felt like an eight-year-old again, in a good way, when talking with Aunt Elizabeth. I guess in your ancestors' eyes you never really grow up. They'll always remember you like a child. We do the same with the once-little ones in our lives.

It was like a movie scene when the camera slowly panned back from the close-up to reveal the entire room-full of people. The soundtrack changed from individual voices to the cluttered hum of many conversations. It was then I realized the weight of the moment.

I am in the same room with every one of my dad's family. All of them, even Grandma and Granddaddy are here with me.

I felt a wave of warmth wash over me, like someone poured a thick layer of fresh molasses over my head. It dripped its way down until it absolutely enveloped my entire being. I knew something wonderful was happening.

As if on cue, everyone in the room turned and looked directly at me. Grandma, Granddaddy, Joe, Jimmy, Charlie, Esther and Elizabeth. It was as if they all knew something I didn't and couldn't wait to tell me.

Their faces were beaming. Like one of those welcome-home scenes in the movies, they slowly stepped back and parted in the middle.

It was then I saw my dad. He was standing right there in the middle of his mom, dad, brothers and sisters. He didn't say a word, but gave me a look that said, "Everything's going to be okay, Son."

Just like that, the room was empty. I was alone in the funeral home chapel. My father's body lay in the casket.

Like the place in between asleep and awake, it took a moment to sink in. The memories were so thick I scooped them up in my hands, held them to my face, and breathed them deeply for a long time. I carry their fragrance to this day.

We have only moments, then memories.

Sparks of Life

Without memory, human beings would truly be a poor species. For some reason, we've been given this amazing gift which allows experiences to remain. People we love, live on long after they've stopped walking the earth. As hurtful as death is, if we fail to recognize this, it robs us of life.

Take some time and look at those old photographs. The ones in the albums and the ones in your mind. Let the bad memories fall away. Don't pick them up again. Hold onto the good ones with all your might. They're all you've got.

This story was written years after every single person in my dad's family was gone. My mother was the last of the in-laws to survive. Now she's gone too. If this is not the case with you, if you've still family left, cherish every single moment you have. If the previous generation is all gone like mine is, cherish every memory—the ones you have, and the ones you're making.

Some perfect tomorrow is complete when surrounded by those we love. By those who love us, all of them. Ancestors and descendants, our tribe in heaven and on earth, surrounded by love.

CHAPTER 34

Wish I
Had You Back Today

"Hey Dad, hey Mom. Here I am ironing a shirt again. Pretty mundane I know, but it made me think of you today. Okay, the fact your portraits were hanging in the same room helped me miss you a little." A burst of steam escaped as the iron pressed a cuff. My left hand got a little too close to the steam plume. Finger straight to mouth. Instinctively. I glanced up at their framed 8x10 portraits.

The classic photographs are such a sweet reminder of who they were. Those famous Olan Mills portraits which often seem plastic and posed. These were posed, but far from plastic. Thanks Olan Mills. You captured my folks' entire personalities in 1/30th of a second.

It was one of those zipadeedoodah days. The sky was so blue you could reach up, grab a handful, and smear it on your palette to use for the "landscape in watercolor" you always planned to paint. A gentle breeze sang through the wind chimes hanging in the Chinaberry tree. Puffy white clouds coasted lazily by. I'm certain a song-laden bluebird landed on my shoulder a few times.

I looked at my mother's portrait on the right. She was dressed in white lace. Her back straight. Smiling eyes warmed anyone she met. Even from her likeness the warmth was there. It brought back a favorite memory from years ago.

We were in her front lawn. Sitting in her faded brown lawn chairs. Splashes of dark pink azaleas provided background. Even now I could almost hear Black Creek swift its way past the dock pilings.

"Mom, I think you're one of those amazing people whose spirit and soul must be cosmically tethered to the weather." I shifted in the chair and crossed my legs.

"Sugar, you know I sometimes barely make it through the cloudy and chilly days." A breeze blew a wisp of hair into her face. She combed it back using her little finger. "I think I only make it by holding on to the hope of the sun's return." Laughed her easy laugh. She looked at me.

"Well, stormy days don't seem to bother me as much." I said. "But these clear days where you can see forever? They plant my feet about six inches off the ground."

In the portrait on the left, Dad was dressed in his best three-piece suit. He was a simple country boy, but always dreamed of having a nice house, a long car, and enough twenties to fill his sterling silver money clip. My memories kept him in light-colored dungarees (forever endeared in our family as "Grandpa Dennis Jeans") and a tight-fitting polo shirt with way too many pens stuffed in the breast pocket.

Seeing him frozen in this framed portrait dressed in his

Sunday best evoked a warm smile. "Gosh, I love you Dad." Sprung from my lips. I turned the shirt around to iron the button side. Gave the steam plume a wide berth this time.

I wanted to fix my eyes on his stately figure. The one with him clutching his jacket's lapel and staring out at me with that debonair Seaton grin. As I did, I knew the "other" photo was there. I tried to convince myself not to look.

Try as I may, my eyes couldn't resist making their way down to the lower left-hand corner of the wood frame. There, as adorned so many of our framed family portraits around the house, a 4x6 print was wedged in front of the glass—a subtle reminder of another slice of life captured on film which somehow related to what lay behind it.

This 4x6 was the very last photo of my dad and me. It was taken a few months before the dastardly disease robbed him from us. In this photo, he was thin. He was jaundiced. He was dying.

"Damn you, Cancer." I caught myself voicing the thought. The words echoed down the hallway. Giving "cancer" an eerie resonance. I didn't mean it as a swear word, popular explicative or figure of speech. It was a sincere and genuine curse.

The number of loved ones prematurely robbed by this single human malady is staggering. No matter the worldwide statistics, (which are alarming) the gritty reality is how this thief affects us personally. Where it truly hits home. My dad. Your mom. His uncle. Her son. Their grandmother.

We all know life on this earth is not forever. Something will eventually be the cause of the end of all our lives. It's just the way things are.

What do we do with these "premature" deaths? How do

we deal with diseases and circumstances which are out of our control? Which take our loved ones from us? We walk.

Walking is something most of us take for granted every single day. It's also nothing less than a miracle of muscle mechanics coupled with countless brain signals. We put one foot in front of the other. We don't lean too much to the right or the left. We keep ourselves about centered. Not too much forward, not too much backward. We balance.

We see the 4x6 of their last image—but we don't let it block the view of the Olan Mills portrait. Focusing too much on one or the other gives an unrealistic view of life.

After the sorrowful anger of losing a loved one subsides, the beauty of the fullness of their lives must propel us to embrace every single moment we have left on Earth. It must.

I finished ironing my shirt, went outside, and sat for a while in the bright blueness of the day. The sun massaged my face with its warm hands. A breeze stroked my hair with its unpredictable fingers. I caught the pleasant smell of something cooking on the neighbor's grill.

I closed my eyes and found myself wishing I had my dad back.

Sparks of Life

We all take life for granted, don't we? We know reality says we'll all die one day. Yet we push the thought to the furthest back of our mind. Forget about dying one day—just remember you are alive right now.

━━━

Anyone who's lived to mid-life has experienced the loss of a loved one. It's only natural to wish you had them back. Hold tightly to what was good about their lives. Toss away the memory of their faults. There's a reason we eulogize and exalt a person as better than they were in life after they're gone. It feels better. Thinking well of someone is good for us too. Makes us nicer people.

━━━

You can't do anything about the ones who've gone on before you. You can let the ones who are alive right here and now know how much you love and appreciate them.

━━━

Some perfect tomorrow wraps itself around a good memory. Incubates it. Nurtures it. Makes it part of who you are. Good memories shape your brain. They shape you. They will change your world. The one you live in now. The one you're building for your children's children.

Afterword

AS WE CLOSE OUR TIME TOGETHER, I'd like you to know I've truly enjoyed sharing these amazing stories with you. The precious people who went through these times in their lives taught me so much.

Any one of them would tell you they'd trade a million lessons learned—lessons taught them by death and grief—for one single moment to be able to hug the one they lost. Just one moment.

Here you go. Take all my lessons-learned back. [hug] Thank you. I love you. I miss you so much.

A wish like this could seem unhealthy. Friends tell us thinking about some ethereal trade-off of life lessons for hugs from the Great Beyond is just ripping the bandage off the wound. I think if we don't have thoughts like this, we may want to take our own pulse.

The amount we grieve is in direct proportion to the amount we love.

I hope you take away what you need from these stories today. There'll be more needs tomorrow. They'll be there. They'll be different from today's, but the needs will continue in some fashion for the rest of your life on Earth.

Your life will never be the same. It can't be. Losing someone you love is losing a part of your very self. And it's not okay.

It is possible to keep walking. Slower gait, different gait. Sometimes painful. Sometimes gruesome. Sometimes even joyful. But you can keep walking.

I've always held to the theory when someone we love dies, our spirit goes into shock. Just like our bodies do when we are physically injured. I call it spiritual shock.

In medical terms, shock is the body's response to a sudden drop in blood pressure. At first, the body responds to this life-threatening situation by constricting blood vessels in the extremities. This is called vasoconstriction and it helps conserve blood flow to the vital organs.

I don't think we'd be able to endure the totality of what death does to us without our minds, spirits and hearts going into spiritual shock to conserve our vital lifeforce.

Loss is too crushing. Too crippling. Too impossible. Even with this protective buffer.

It's a different world in which we live today. It seems to change daily, sometimes hourly. Customs, traditions, values —some are concrete, some are more fluid. Even in a different world, there is still light which shines in darkness. There are still those who really care.

Those who are hurting, who have lost a lot. They have mourned and are working through what grief looks like. Yet they keep walking—even helping others around them.

Walking. Helping. Grieving. Loving. Living.

People who make us proud to be called human beings. I think you're one of them.

We are amazing creatures, we humans. We are often at our best when things are at their worst. I believe since you've been through your worst you still have some of your best yet to go. Go you shall.

Some perfect tomorrow is a true force. A force which propels us. Drives us to accomplish great things. Great advancements. From landing on Mars—to cuddling a sick child in our arms. It is hope in its clearest form. Hope for a better future. A better you. A better us.

May God bless you and may you have peace. Every day. Every moment. Every breath.

The yellow Adirondack chair is a symbol of hope.
Share this hope with someone you care about:

Give them your copy of *Some Perfect Tomorrow.*

Then—tell us your story.

CRAIGSEATON.COM

About the Author

A freelance writer, performing musician, and award-winning songwriter, Craig R. Seaton has also helped thousands of families with the often-overwhelming details surrounding funeral, cremation, and burial arrangements.

Coupled with a poignant worldview, Craig's professional and personal experiences with death give him the ability to communicate words of comfort and wisdom. He engages his readers with thought-provoking stories about life, love, and family.

Former 1970s lead singer and keyboard player, Craig now appears as a guest musician and vocalist at many events. He performs Golden Oldies concerts for senior centers, nursing homes, assisted living facilities and senior living communities.

Craig's writing has been featured in the premier national funeral directors' magazine, *Southern Calls* and the popular e-magazine, *Thursday Review*. He's written many articles about life and death for his local community newspapers, and blogs for his website: craigseaton.com.

He's an accomplished public speaker and has been featured on the Investigation Discovery Channel television series, *Blood Relatives* as a grief professional.

A US Navy veteran, Craig lives in Florida with his wife, Tami. He has two adult children: son, Tylor, daughter, Tara—and some of the most beautiful grandchildren you've ever laid eyes on.

CPSIA information can be obtained
at www.ICGtesting.com
Printed in the USA
LVHW090730130621
690102LV00003B/459